"The One Page Business Plan
does something outrageous!
It causes very busy people
to stop and think.
As they start to write...
it confirms both their clarity
and their confusion!"

— Jim Horan
President
The One Page Business Plan Company

WARNING – DISCLAIMER

This book was designed to provide information in regard to the subject matter covered. It is not the purpose of this manual to reprint all of the information available to the author/publisher, but to complement, amplify and supplement other sources.

Use of The One Page Business Plan® does not in any way guarantee the success of an idea or organization, nor does it ensure that financing will be made available. When legal or expert assistance is required, the services of a competent professional should be sought.

The author/publisher shall have neither liability nor responsibility to any person or entity with respect to any loss or damage caused, or alleged to be caused, directly or indirectly by the information contained in this book.

If you do not wish to be bound by the above, you may return this book to the publisher for a full refund.

Published by:

The One Page Business Plan Company
1798 Fifth Street
Berkeley, CA 94710
Phone: (510) 705-8400
Fax: (510) 705-8403
www.onepagebusinessplan.com

ISBN-13: 978-1-891315-15-2

FIRST EDITION - v.1.0

Printed in the United States of America

The One Page
Business Plan®

for the Busy Executive

*The Fastest, Easiest Way
to Write a Business Plan!*

By Jim Horan

"*You must
simplify.
You must make
the complex simple,
then you must
make it work.*"

— I.M. Pei
Master Architect

Author's Note

Jim Horan

The One Page Business Plan is much more than a simple planning process. It is a framework for continuously moving your business to the next level of discipline.

The next level of discipline in thinking, communication, decision making, execution and accountability.

This process requires rigorous, strategic thinking. It demands clear and precise communications. The simple questions we use to facilitate the creation of One Page Business Plans require mindful, precise, strategic answers.

One Page Plans facilitate solid decision making. The process distills out what is not critical and strategic...leaving only the most significant aspects of the blueprint for critical review, dialog and decision. There is no room for fluff or filler on a One Page Plan.

The One Page Business Plan has been used by busy owners, executives and their management teams since 1994. This process is proven. It always creates the next level of clarity and focus.

Everyone on your team can write a plan on a single page. They will need encouragement and coaching from you; possibly assistance from an outside professional. You should be able to create a set of one-page plans for your entire company in approximately four weeks; most managers should be able complete an initial draft in 90 minutes to two hours. Most plans will require two to three rounds of edits to be solid. Do not rush the process. Writing is difficult for almost everybody.

Do not complicate this process. It is simple, keep it that way. Getting your best thinking onto a single page will require rigorous thinking, dialog and debate...but for a relatively short period of time.

Most plans fail because they are not implemented. Commit to monitoring the implementation of your One Page Business Plans. Have a monthly meeting whose sole purpose is to review results and progress.

One Page Plans create a culture of discipline. Keep the process transparent and inclusive. Use it to create team cohesion and accountability. You, your team and your business will be stronger!!

Jim Horan
Founder & President, The One Page Business Plan Company

Foreword

What the world's leading author of business best-sellers is saying about The One Page Business Plan®...

"The One Page Business Plan is an out-and-out winner. Period.

It makes great sense to me as a so-called business thinker. But the acid test was applying it to a start-up I co-founded. We spent several days drafting our one pager - and have been editing it ever since. It is a powerful, living document; the very nature of which has led us to important new insights.

The One Page Business Plan = the proverbial better mouse trap!"

- Tom Peters
author of
Leadership,
Re-imagine!,
In Search of Excellence,
Thriving on Chaos,
The Pursuit of Wow!,
and The Circle of Innovation

What Others Are Saying

The One Page Business Plan® takes a complex process and makes it simple!

GAMA International used the One Page Plan process to turn a four inch stack of research, surveys and reports, first into a laser sharp five-year strategic plan, then one-year plans for every department and committee. Every executive would benefit from running their business with this level of precision.
Jeff Hughes
Chief Executive Officer, GAMA International
Washington, DC

"Want to start a business? Grow a brand? Be profitable? First step is to develop a business plan and then communicate it like crazy to everyone. The One Page Business Plan is a great tool...it demands focus and clarity. Everyone on your team should have one!"
Kathy Tierney
Executive Vice Chairman/Immediate Past CEO, Sur La Table
Healdsburg, CA

If there is no plan, there is chaos. The One Page Business Plan looks deceptively simple, but it is in fact an incredibly effective process that creates orderly fashion and accountability out of chaos and dysfunctionality. One Page Plans clearly and concisely document the change that needs to happen.
Chuck Longanecker
President, Business Development Systems
Sacramento, CA

A biz plan is an absolute must. While eventually you need it to "sell" your idea to others, the first person you need to convince is yourself! If you cannot convince yourself you will NOT be able to convince others."
Maxine Clark,
Founder & Chief Executive Bear, Build-A-Bear Workshop®
Saint Louis, MO

For years my annual business plan consisted simply of a set of objectives. The one-page business plan format forced me to think through each objective and create a strategy and action steps that align with the objectives and strategies. The web-based tracking system brought alignment and accountability to our results. Along with the vision and mission statement, the one-page plan is concise yet comprehensive.
Jeff Plummer
Managing Partner, John Hancock Financial Network
Charlotte, NC

The One Page Planning method, along with the web-based tools and software, are great ways to help managers stay strategic even though their days may be spent working primarily on tactical issues."
PJ Anderson
CEO, Herman Miller (San Francisco Franchise)
San Francisco, California

I've never seen a better way to deploy an organization's purpose and business plans than with this brilliant, simple, straightforward approach to planning and performance management. This company's tools, processes, software and consultants are the best of the best!
Frank Tiedemann
CEO, Children's Hospital & Research Center
Oakland, CA

VISION
MISSION
OBJECTIVES
STRATEGIES
ACTION PLANS

Table of Contents

VISION

MISSION

OBJECTIVES

STRATEGIES

ACTION PLANS

Introduction

What is a One Page Business Plan?

"Planning is a process... not an event!

One Page Plans are living, changing, evolving documents!"

The One Page Business Plan is an innovative approach to business planning that captures the essence of any business, project or program on a single page using key words and short phrases.

Most companies use the process to create not only the company's overall plan, but also to create plans for each supporting department, project and program. Since the creation of The One Page Business Plan in 1994, over 500,000 companies have successfully used the process to bring structure, alignment and accountability to their organizations.

The flexible methodology makes it possible for entrepreneurs, business owners, executives, managers and professionals in every organization to have a plan. The standard format makes it easy to review, compare and understand plans.

One Page Business Plans work because:

- Plans actually get documented
- Plans are understandable
- Plans are easy to write, easy to update
- Every manager or team has one

The process creates:

- Alignment
- Accountability
- Results

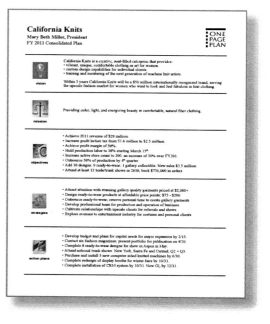

Our Observations...

Why One Page?

You are busy; your time is limited. You need to be clear and focused. You are action and results oriented. Most of us are not good at prose writing... it takes too long to write a well-written sentence, paragraph, page or chapter - and far too long to read. People need to be able to read a plan in about five minutes. They want the essence... the key points. Then they want to talk... to ask clarifying questions, come to agreement... and then take action.

Why Plan?

Most people write plans because they either want or need to achieve different or better results. Plans are blueprints; they describe what is going to be built, how it will be done, and by whom... and the results to be measured.

Why Written Plans?

The spoken word is too fluid; we have a tendency to ramble. When we speak, we almost never say it exactly the same way twice... frequently we forget to share some of the most important details... or spend too much time on the unimportant things. When we write, we choose our words more carefully. Writing takes time, usually much more than talk. The written word requires a higher level of mindfulness and attention to detail. The written word also produces a contract with yourself and others that can be reread, refined... a source for reflection and mindful change if necessary.

Asking simple questions works!

People love to talk about their business! They can easily answer questions like, what are you building, what will your business look like in three years, what has made your business successful to date, what are the critical business development projects and programs you have underway or planned, what do you measure to know if you are on track... and of course, why does your business exist?

The Power is in 5 Key Questions!

Business plan terminology is problematic. Depending on where you went to school, and the companies/organizations you have worked for... the terms Vision, Mission, Objectives, Strategies and Plans probably mean something different to you than the person sitting next to you. We have learned that business planning "definitions" just don't work. We have refined our questions over 15 years with hundreds of thousands of business executives. The five questions we will teach you are simple, easy to remember and they will help get your business plan out of your head and onto paper.

About Planning Processes

Starting with a blank page wastes valuable time!

The examples and the fill-in-the-blank prompts are learning aids… designed to help you quickly learn and master the One Page Business Plan technique. We have learned that most people learn by seeing examples, so we give you lots of them.

The dreaded "writer's block" can easily be eliminated by the use of our proprietary fill-in-the-blank templates. They make the creation of any portion of your business plan easy. Use the fill-in-the-blank templates to quickly capture your thoughts and create the first draft. You will also find that the extensive list of templates can spark your thinking and make sure that you give consideration to your "total" business.

Everyone on your team can and should write a One Page Business Plan!

Have partners? Employees? The number one issue business owners and executives share with us is that they need people to work on the right things… and achieve specific results! Partners complain they are not on the same page! There is a simple solution: have your partners, associates, strategic alliance partners, managers and paid staff create One Page Business Plans for their businesses, profit centers, departments, projects or programs. Do not assume they are executing your plan. Have them create their own!

Final Thought: Plans are important… Execution is critical!

Executives invest in planning because they want and need results. Plans are valuable because they provide the blueprint for where you are taking your business and how you will get there… but ultimately the plans are only as good as the execution. Establish processes such as the scorecard tracking and monthly progress reviews to monitor the implementation of your plans.

Business Plan Terminology is Confusing

There are no universally acceptable definitions to the terms Vision, Mission, Objectives, Strategies or Action Plans. How you use these terms depends entirely on what school you went to and for what companies you have worked. Many companies never successfully complete their business plans because they cannot agree on the basic terminology. We solved the problem!

We translated the five standard business plan elements into five simple and universal questions:

Vision: What are you building?

Mission: Why does this business exist?

Objectives: What business results will you measure?

Strategies: How will you build this business?

Action Plans: What is the work to be done?

Writing a business plan for a department or program?

Modify the Mission and Strategy questions by replacing the word "business" with "department" or "program":

Department Usage	Program Usage
Mission: Why does this department exist?	Mission: Why does this program exist?
Strategy: How will you build this department?	Strategy: How will you build this program?

Business Plans Can be Simple and Clean

The best way to understand The One Page Business Plan is to read one... One Page Business Plans can generally be read in about five minutes or less.

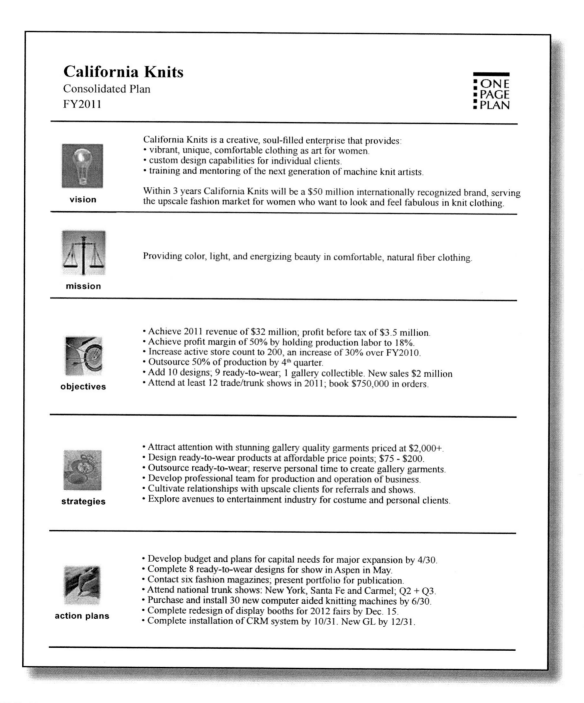

California Knits
Consolidated Plan
FY2011

▪ ONE
▪ PAGE
▪ PLAN

vision

California Knits is a creative, soul-filled enterprise that provides:
• vibrant, unique, comfortable clothing as art for women.
• custom design capabilities for individual clients.
• training and mentoring of the next generation of machine knit artists.

Within 3 years California Knits will be a $50 million internationally recognized brand, serving the upscale fashion market for women who want to look and feel fabulous in knit clothing.

mission

Providing color, light, and energizing beauty in comfortable, natural fiber clothing.

objectives

• Achieve 2011 revenue of $32 million; profit before tax of $3.5 million.
• Achieve profit margin of 50% by holding production labor to 18%.
• Increase active store count to 200, an increase of 30% over FY2010.
• Outsource 50% of production by 4th quarter.
• Add 10 designs; 9 ready-to-wear; 1 gallery collectible. New sales $2 million
• Attend at least 12 trade/trunk shows in 2011; book $750,000 in orders.

strategies

• Attract attention with stunning gallery quality garments priced at $2,000+.
• Design ready-to-wear products at affordable price points; $75 - $200.
• Outsource ready-to-wear; reserve personal time to create gallery garments.
• Develop professional team for production and operation of business.
• Cultivate relationships with upscale clients for referrals and shows.
• Explore avenues to entertainment industry for costume and personal clients.

action plans

• Develop budget and plans for capital needs for major expansion by 4/30.
• Complete 8 ready-to-wear designs for show in Aspen in May.
• Contact six fashion magazines; present portfolio for publication.
• Attend national trunk shows: New York, Santa Fe and Carmel; Q2 + Q3.
• Purchase and install 30 new computer aided knitting machines by 6/30.
• Complete redesign of display booths for 2012 fairs by Dec. 15.
• Complete installation of CRM system by 10/31. New GL by 12/31.

The One Page Business Plan has Many Uses

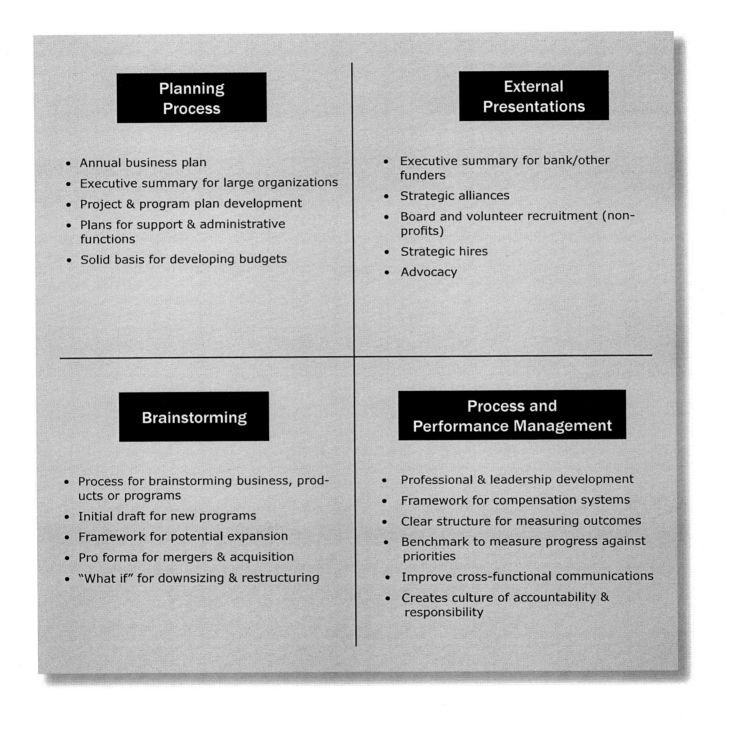

Planning Process

- Annual business plan
- Executive summary for large organizations
- Project & program plan development
- Plans for support & administrative functions
- Solid basis for developing budgets

External Presentations

- Executive summary for bank/other funders
- Strategic alliances
- Board and volunteer recruitment (non-profits)
- Strategic hires
- Advocacy

Brainstorming

- Process for brainstorming business, products or programs
- Initial draft for new programs
- Framework for potential expansion
- Pro forma for mergers & acquisition
- "What if" for downsizing & restructuring

Process and Performance Management

- Professional & leadership development
- Framework for compensation systems
- Clear structure for measuring outcomes
- Benchmark to measure progress against priorities
- Improve cross-functional communications
- Creates culture of accountability & responsibility

How to Use This Book and CD

The primary purpose of this book is to help you get your plan onto paper. It has been carefully crafted to capture the plan that is in your head.

Carry this book with you, write in it, use it as a container for capturing your thoughts as they occur. If you have multiple businesses, partners or managers, have them get their own copy.

It's not necessary to do all the exercises in this book. If you can write your One Page Business Plan by reviewing the samples — skip the exercises. They are there to help guide you through the process if you need help.

Do not underestimate the power of the questions that appear simple! They are simple by design. If you do not get an "aha" from them, have somebody ask you the questions. Important insights may begin to flow.

This book is divided into nine sections with the focus on the five elements of The One Page Business Plan. You can start anywhere. It's OK to jump around!

There are many different ways to use and interact with this book. Exercises can be done:

- by oneself

- with a planning partner (2 or more executives or business owners)

- as a management team

- as a group

- at a retreat or conference

- with a licensed One Page Business Plan consultant

 The Executive Tool Kit CD at the back of the book contains The One Page Business Plan templates, bonus exercises, budget worksheet, plus scorecards for monitoring and tracking your results.

Assessments

What's working? What's not?

"Too many people over plan and under execute.

Plan for what is critical... then execute your plan."

Intuitively you know the status of your business, profit center, project or program... but when was the last time you stopped and gave it a checkup? Took a real look under the hood?

This section has four 10 Point Assessments to help you quickly determine what is working in your company, and what isn't. We've also included a 10 Point Personal Assessment for you to do a little personal checkup, if you so desire.

These assessments are designed to help you quickly take the pulse of your business, which areas are strong, which aspects need attention. As with all of the exercises in this book, they are meant to be done quickly, relying on your intuition, state of mind and frankly, what is keeping you up at night and/or making you smile.

We encourage you not to overwork these assessments. In our workshops we give participants about five minutes to do the overall business assessment.

It's possible that not all of the categories on the 10 Point Assessments will apply to your business; if so, you have two choices: 1) ignore those that do not apply; 2) modify the category to reflect an area of your business that is critical to your success and then rate your performance.

As you work through your plan, be sure to come back to these assessments to ensure your plan addresses the key issues you identify here.

What's Working in Your Business? What's Not?

Step 1: Rate each of these elements on a scale of 1 to 10; 1 = disaster, 10 = brilliantly successful
Step 2: On the following page identify the key elements/issues that influenced your rating.
Step 3: On the following page make note of what needs to be changed to correct the problem areas.

1. Sales	N/A 1 2 3 4 5 6 7 8 9 10
2. Profitability	N/A 1 2 3 4 5 6 7 8 9 10
3. Cash Flow	N/A 1 2 3 4 5 6 7 8 9 10
4. Planning & Budgets	N/A 1 2 3 4 5 6 7 8 9 10
5. Expense Control	N/A 1 2 3 4 5 6 7 8 9 10
6. Marketing & New Products	N/A 1 2 3 4 5 6 7 8 9 10
7. Technology	N/A 1 2 3 4 5 6 7 8 9 10
8. Employees & Subcontractors	N/A 1 2 3 4 5 6 7 8 9 10
9. Strategic Alliances/Vendors	N/A 1 2 3 4 5 6 7 8 9 10
10. Quality & Safety	N/A 1 2 3 4 5 6 7 8 9 10
Overall Assessment	**1 2 3 4 5 6 7 8 9 10**

Step 4: As you develop your plan, be sure to come back to this page to address the issues identified here.

Where are the Opportunities for Improvement?

In left column: Identify key issues or opportunities that influenced your assessment.
In right column: Brainstorm actions that can be taken to improve low ratings or maintain high ratings.

Key Issue or Opportunity	Action to Improve or Maintain
Example: Poor Sales	More phone contact with existing clients, less emphasis on collateral, more listening, offer better solutions

Your Sales/Marketing Programs: What's Working?

Step 1: Rate each of these elements on a scale of 1 to 10; 1 = disaster, 10 = brilliantly successful
Step 2: On the following page identify the key elements/issues that influenced your rating.
Step 3: On the following page make note of what needs to be changed to correct the problem areas.

1. Know & Understand our Ideal Client	N/A	1	2	3	4	5	6	7	8	9	10
2. Compelling Product & Service Offerings	N/A	1	2	3	4	5	6	7	8	9	10
3. Effective Marketing System that Attracts our Ideal Clients	N/A	1	2	3	4	5	6	7	8	9	10
4. Pricing Policies that Attract Ideal Clients & Produce Excellent Margins	N/A	1	2	3	4	5	6	7	8	9	10
5. Effective Customer Service Systems	N/A	1	2	3	4	5	6	7	8	9	10
6. Strong Strategic Alliances	N/A	1	2	3	4	5	6	7	8	9	10
7. Effective Advertising, Promotions, Events, Seminars	N/A	1	2	3	4	5	6	7	8	9	10
8. Compelling Web Site & Collateral Materials	N/A	1	2	3	4	5	6	7	8	9	10
9. Sales & Marketing Activity Tracking Systems	N/A	1	2	3	4	5	6	7	8	9	10
10. Effective Project & Cost Controls	N/A	1	2	3	4	5	6	7	8	9	10
Overall Assessment		1	2	3	4	5	6	7	8	9	10

Step 4: As you develop your plan, be sure to come back to this page to address the issues identified here.

THE ONE PAGE BUSINESS PLAN

Where are the Opportunities for Improvement?

In left column: Identify key issues or opportunities that influenced your assessment.
In right column: Brainstorm actions that can be taken to improve low ratings or maintain high ratings.

Key Issue or Opportunity	Action to Improve or Maintain

Example for Advertising, Promos, Events:

Local advertising and promotions producing too few leads

Move to more personal forms of business development like seminars & special events. More contact with existing customers

Planning & Controls: What's Working?

Step 1: Rate each of these management processes; 1 = disaster, 10 = brilliantly successful
Step 2: On the following page identify the key elements/issues that influenced your rating.
Step 3: On the following page note of what needs to be changed to correct the problem areas.

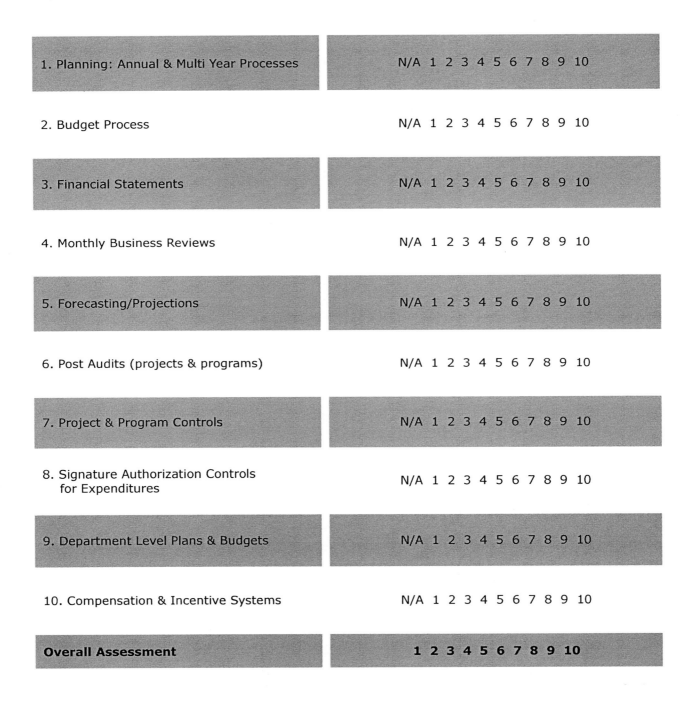

1. Planning: Annual & Multi Year Processes	N/A 1 2 3 4 5 6 7 8 9 10
2. Budget Process	N/A 1 2 3 4 5 6 7 8 9 10
3. Financial Statements	N/A 1 2 3 4 5 6 7 8 9 10
4. Monthly Business Reviews	N/A 1 2 3 4 5 6 7 8 9 10
5. Forecasting/Projections	N/A 1 2 3 4 5 6 7 8 9 10
6. Post Audits (projects & programs)	N/A 1 2 3 4 5 6 7 8 9 10
7. Project & Program Controls	N/A 1 2 3 4 5 6 7 8 9 10
8. Signature Authorization Controls for Expenditures	N/A 1 2 3 4 5 6 7 8 9 10
9. Department Level Plans & Budgets	N/A 1 2 3 4 5 6 7 8 9 10
10. Compensation & Incentive Systems	N/A 1 2 3 4 5 6 7 8 9 10
Overall Assessment	**1 2 3 4 5 6 7 8 9 10**

Step 4: As you develop your plan, be sure to come back to this page to address the issues identified here.

Where are the Opportunities for Improvement?

In left column: Identify key areas that influenced your assessment.
In right column: Brainstorm actions that can be taken to improve low ratings or maintain high ratings.

Problem Areas or Successes	Action to Improve or Maintain

Example for Post Audit:
Internal controls on spending are weak.

Can develop and implement budgeting at department level. Carefully monitor variances monthly.

Financial Health Assessment

Step 1: Rate each of these management processes; 1 = disaster, 10 = brilliantly successful
Step 2: On the following page identify the key elements/issues that influenced your rating.
Step 3: On the following page make note of what needs to be changed to correct the problem areas.

1. Working capital	N/A 1 2 3 4 5 6 7 8 9 10
2. Gross margins	N/A 1 2 3 4 5 6 7 8 9 10
3. Pricing, discounts, promotions	N/A 1 2 3 4 5 6 7 8 9 10
4. Cost of sales: product/service/programs	N/A 1 2 3 4 5 6 7 8 9 10
5. Operating Costs	N/A 1 2 3 4 5 6 7 8 9 10
6. Profit before tax	N/A 1 2 3 4 5 6 7 8 9 10
7. Accounts receivables	N/A 1 2 3 4 5 6 7 8 9 10
8. Inventories	N/A 1 2 3 4 5 6 7 8 9 10
9. Bank relationships/loan convenants	N/A 1 2 3 4 5 6 7 8 9 10
10. Debt	N/A 1 2 3 4 5 6 7 8 9 10
Overall Assessment	**1 2 3 4 5 6 7 8 9 10**

Step 4: As you develop your plan, be sure to come back to this page to address the issues identified here.

Where are the Opportunities for Improvement?

In left column: Identify key areas that influenced your assessment.
In right column: Brainstorm actions that can be taken to improve low ratings or maintain high ratings.

Problem Areas or Successes	Action to Improve or Maintain

Example for Post Audit:

Internal controls on spending are weak.

Can develop and implement budgeting at department level. Carefully monitor variances monthly.

How are you? A Personal Assessment

Step 1: Rate each of these elements on a scale of 1 to 10; 1 = disaster, 10 = brilliantly successful
Step 2: On the following page identify the key elements/issues that influenced your rating.
Step 3: On the following page make note of what needs to be changed to correct the problem areas.

1. Your Physical Health	N/A 1 2 3 4 5 6 7 8 9 10
2. Your Mental Health	N/A 1 2 3 4 5 6 7 8 9 10
3. Relationships at Work	N/A 1 2 3 4 5 6 7 8 9 10
4. Your Role at Work	N/A 1 2 3 4 5 6 7 8 9 10
5. Personal Finances	N/A 1 2 3 4 5 6 7 8 9 10
6. Life Outside of Work	N/A 1 2 3 4 5 6 7 8 9 10
7. Sense of Community	N/A 1 2 3 4 5 6 7 8 9 10
8. Plans for Retirement	N/A 1 2 3 4 5 6 7 8 9 10
9. Stress Level	N/A 1 2 3 4 5 6 7 8 9 10
10. Sense of Well Being	N/A 1 2 3 4 5 6 7 8 9 10
Overall Assessment	**1 2 3 4 5 6 7 8 9 10**

Step 4: As you develop your plan, be sure to come back to this page to address the issues identified here.

Where are the Opportunities for Improvement?

In left column: Identify key issues or opportunities that influenced your assessment.
In right column: Brainstorm actions that can be taken to improve low ratings or maintain high ratings.

Key Issue or Opportunity	Action to Improve or Maintain

Example for Life Outside Work:

Not having enough fun! Need some downtime!

Consider taking Mondays off, or every other Monday. Need time to rejuvenate. Spend time on the boat with family.

The Vision Statement
What are you building?

Everybody is building something... a company, an organization, a department, professional practice, a non-profit*. Well-written Vision Statements answer the question: What is being built?... in three sentences or less!

The question for you is what are you building? What do you want your business to look like in 1, 3 or 5 years? An effective Vision Statement need not be long, but it must clearly describe what you are building. A few key words will go a long way.

Vision Statements answer these questions:

- What type of business is this?
- What markets does it serve?
- What is the geographic scope?
- Where will the business be located?
- Who are the target customers?
- What are the key products and services?
- How big will the company be... and when?
- What will revenues be?
- Will it have employees? How many?

Almost everyone has a Vision for their company, but some are better at articulating it. Many people struggle with capturing their Vision effectively in writing. At The One Page Business Plan Company we have learned that with a little prompting, most entrepreneurs, business professionals, executives and owners can capture the essence of their Vision in just a few minutes.

If you are building a non-profit you will find The One Page Business Plan for Non-Profit Organizations to be very helpful. This book was created specifically for non-profits and is full of non-profit sample plans.

A Simple Formula for Writing a Vision Statement...

Type of business
+
Geographic Scope & Projected Annual Sales
+
Core Products/Services
+
Customer Profile

Here are some examples using this formula:

Ezme Designs	Within the next 5 years, grow Ezme Designs into a successful international ceramics, housewares and lifestyle company, with annual sales of $15 million providing unique, handmade, quality designs of tableware, jewelry and sculptural ceramics to art conscious men and women, retail stores, catalogs, craft galleries and internet shoppers.
Harps, Etc.	Within the next 3 years grow Harps, Etc. into a $20 million international harp sales and accessories retail franchise company providing new and used harps for sales, rental franchisevand instruction, plus accessories and services to professionals, students, teachers and aficionados of the harp.
Suit Your Fancy	Within the next 2 years grow Suit Your Fancy into a $500 million, successful national home-based party-plan retail sales business providing high quality stylish and comfortable women's clothing and offering valuable entrepreneurial opportunities to incredibly motivated women in all ages and stages of life desiring to create their own business successes.
East Way Yoga	Within the next 3 years grow East Way Yoga into a $10 million Northern California provider of on-site workplace yoga classes, inspiring companies and their employees to create a satisfying and fulfilling work/life experience by transforming their moment-to-moment awareness. We will also create and sell new yoga-related DVDs locally and online to support the ongoing practice of living life more fully through yoga.

Crafting a Vision Statement

Getting the first draft onto paper is always the most difficult. It is infinitely easier to edit! The fill-in-the-blank-template below is geared to help you quickly create a first draft. Each blank in essence is a question; complete all the blanks, and you create a first draft... quickly and easily! Not able to fill in all of the blanks at this time? Don't worry... complete those that you can! Revisit the blanks later, you may need to do some research or enlist help from others.

Vision Statement

Within the next _____ years grow _____ into a $_____

                      (company name)   (est. annual sales)

_____ _____ company providing

    (geographic scope)   (type of business)
    (local/region/nat'l/int'l)

_____

            (list 2-3 of your most successful products/services)

to _____

       (list 2-3 characteristics of your ideal clients/customers)

The following Vision Statement was created using the fill-in-the-blanks template and then edited. It is brief, but very clear.

> In the next 3 years, grow VHS Engineering into a $350 million international wireless technology solutions provider capable of designing, building, and hosting leading edge wireless products and networks throughout North America for corporations with a minimum of 1000 employees.

This exercise is designed to help you brainstorm the Who, What, Why, When, Where and Hows for your business. Review the questions, write down your initial thoughts, insights and ahas. Writing outside the boxes is allowed and encouraged.

WHAT?

Services or products? or both? How many?

Company image: What will this company be known for?

Owner's Role: What is your role? How will you spend your time?

WHERE?

Company: Local, regional, national, or international?

Clients/Recipients: Where are they? What cities, states, countries?

Business Operations: Headquarters, offices, program locations, etc.?

WHO?

Customers: Who are they? What needs do they have?

Staff: Who needs to be on your team? When

Strategic Alliances: Who can you partner with?

Advisors: Who can provide professional and strategic advice and help you grow this business properly?

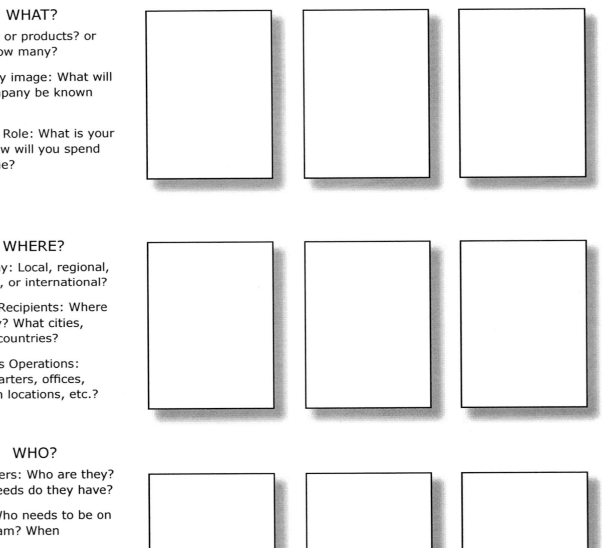

Creating the Business You Want

Don't worry about answering all of the questions; they may or may not apply to your business.

WHEN?

Start-up: When will this business be operational?

Facilities: When will office/manufacturing/distribution space be required?

Systems: When must they be selected, tested, and operational?

WHY?

Owner: Why am I creating this business?

Customers/Clients: Why will they buy these products or services?

Investors/Bankers: Why will they fund this business?

HOW?

Funding: How will this business be funded?

Culture: How do you want to interact with customers, employees, vendors?

Personal Beliefs: How will your personal beliefs impact this business?

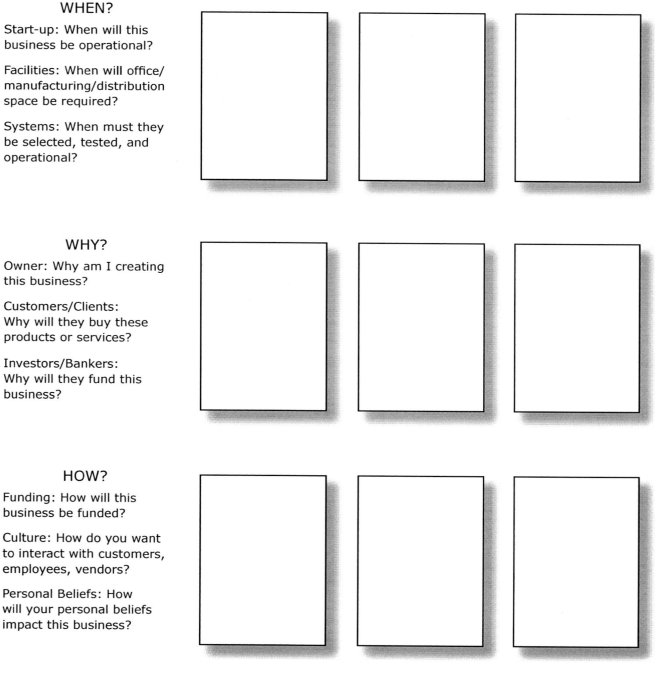

Crafting a Vision Statement for a Department*

If your company has support functions, have each of your managers create a Vision Statement for their department. This template will make creating the first draft easy.

Department Vision Statement Template

Within the next _____ years grow _____ at _____
      (1, 3, or 5 yrs)   (department name)   (company name)

into a successful provider of _____
                        (describe services and/or functions)

to _____. Future capabilities/capacity
          (name internal/external customers)

will include _____.
                (describe capabilities/capacity)

*For larger/established companies

Department Vision Statements that Work Together

Well written Vision Statements at the department level answer the question, "What will this department look like in 1, 3, or 5 years?" The Vision Statements should provide a sense of the services and/or function that the department will be providing within the planning horizon indicated.

Here is an example of a set of integrated Vision Statements for one company:

Consolidated Plan	Within the next 3 years, build a $150 million global wireless applications solutions company serving the financial services, health care and transportation industries.
Sales	Within the next 18 months, build a national external sales department consisting of 20 senior sales reps focused on large custom system sales supported by a highly effective telemarketing function with 6 specialists selling packaged products & limited consulting services.
Marketing	Over the next 3 years, expand Marketing to include market research, product development & marketing communications depts.; total staff: 10 professionals + 5 support. Continue to outsource PR & Advertising.
Engineering & Technology	Over the next 3 years, build a state-of-the-art technology center with an engineering team of 30 professionals capable of designing, building, & hosting leading edge wireless products and services.
Human Resources	Build a highly motivated and effective global workforce of non-union employees and independent contractors to support a rapidly growing company. Internal HR staff will consist of 6 employees.
Accounting & Finance	Build highly efficient accounting system/function that seamlessly integrates all of the business' financial, operational, customer & management processes. Total head count in 3 years of 20.

Feedback Exercise

Reflect on your Vision Statement for a few days. Then consider sharing your Vision Statement with at least 2-4 people and asking them for their feedback. Use this page to take notes.

First Person Feedback

Second Person Feedback

Note here key words and phrases from above or other sources you would like to use in your own Vision Statement:

Next Steps for Your Vision Statement

1 **REVIEW:** Does your Vision Statement answer these questions?

VISION STATEMENT QUESTIONS:	YES/NO
What type of business is this?	
What markets does it serve?	
What is the geographic scope?	
Where will the business be located?	
Who are the target customers?	
What are the key products and services?	
How big will the company be... and when?	
What will revenues be?	
Will it have employees? How many?	

2 **REFLECT:** Assuming the reader knows nothing about your business, does your Vision Statement clearly answer the question: *What are you building? Ask yourself... Is this the business I want to build?*

3 **SHARE:** After reflecting on your Vision Statement for a few days, consider sharing your Vision Statement with 2-4 people and asking them for feedback.

4 **COMPLETION!:** Satisfied with your Vision Statement? Go to the CD at the back of the book, find The One Page Business Plan template in the Forms and Templates folder, and type your Vision Statement into the template.

VISION
MISSION
OBJECTIVES
STRATEGIES
ACTION PLANS

Mission

Why does this business exist?

Mission Statements always answer the question, "Who will we serve and what will we do for them?"

Every business exists for a reason. Can you describe why your business exists in 8 – 12 words? Can your executives and their managers describe why their departments, projects and programs exist...in a compelling way?

The best Mission Statements are short, memorable, frequently have an emotional element and are always catalytic. They attract customers who want to buy what you have to sell. They attract employees who want to work for your company because they understand who you are, what you do, your values and they know they will fit in.

Great Mission Statements are critical for attracting the right type of vendors and investors; donors and volunteers if your organization is a non-profit.

Mission Statements for staff and support functions remind your employees their job exists to be in service of their internal clients...departments that are relying on them to provide very specific services.

Well crafted Mission Statements have always been an integral part of a company's branding strategy that compels customers to buy, but the same Mission Statements should influence all significant business and management decisions.

Mission Statements answer these specific questions:

- Why does this business exist?
- What are we committed to providing to our customers?
- What promise are we making to our clients?
- What wants, needs, desires, pain, or problems do our products and services solve?
- What is our unique selling proposition?

A Simple Formula for Writing a Mission Statement...

> *Ideal Client Description*
> +
> *Goal/Benefit of your Products/Services*

Here are some examples using this formula, and others that do not follow the formula...but are very powerful in answering the question, "Why does this business exist?"

Nike	Inspire Every Athlete in the World!
Google	We organize the world's information and make it universally accessible and useful!
LensCrafters	Helping people see better one hour at a time
West Marine	We make boating fun!
Nature Conservancy	Helping to save the last great places on earth.
Safeway	Ingredients for Life!
Ethan Allen	We create beautiful spaces!
History Channel	Where history comes alive!
UCSF, a teaching hospital	Caring, Healing, Teaching and Discovery

Crafting Your Mission Statement

Use the fill-in-the-blank template below to create a first draft of your Mission Statement. Experiment with variations until you come up with a short, powerful, memorable statement that describes your ideal clients and how you serve them. The best Mission Statements are 8-12 words.

Why does this business exist?

1st Attempt:

We help _____ _____.
            (recipient of your products/services)   (goal or benefit of your products/services)

2nd Attempt:

3rd Attempt:

brainstorm
EXERCISE

Who Do You Want to be in Service of?

Believe it or not... you have a choice as to who you work with! Consider these questions:

- Who do you want to work with?
- What causes/issues are important to you?
- What problems can you solve?
- Who is currently working with your ideal client?

- Where are the people you want to serve?
- What work gives you professional satisfaction?
- Who has the resources to pay your fees?
- Who makes you smile?

Exercise instructions:

1. In the center circle, describe the people, groups or organizations you want to work with. These people have faces! What do they look like? What do they need help with? The more specific you can be... the easier it will be for you to find them, and vice-versa.

2. In the outer circle, list the people and/or communities that know your existing and/or future clients. These people need to know you exist; they can introduce you to those that need your service.

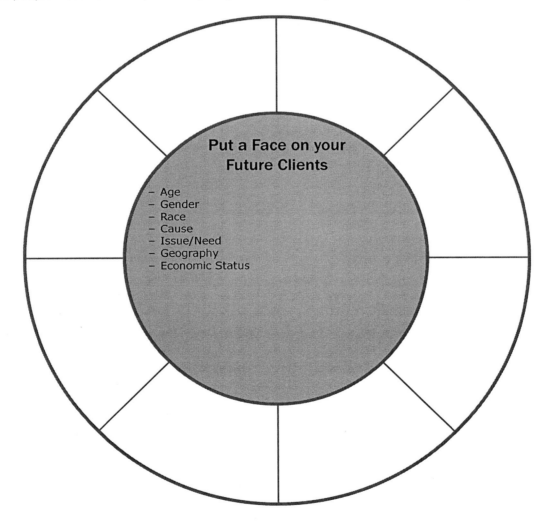

Put a Face on your Future Clients

- Age
- Gender
- Race
- Cause
- Issue/Need
- Geography
- Economic Status

When you are clear about who you want to serve, you make it easier for them to find you!

And Why?

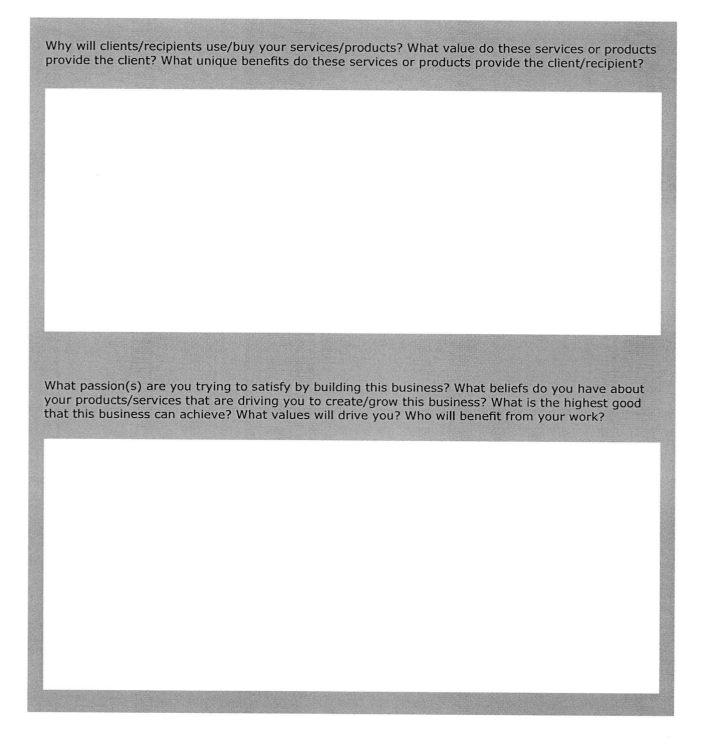

Why will clients/recipients use/buy your services/products? What value do these services or products provide the client? What unique benefits do these services or products provide the client/recipient?

What passion(s) are you trying to satisfy by building this business? What beliefs do you have about your products/services that are driving you to create/grow this business? What is the highest good that this business can achieve? What values will drive you? Who will benefit from your work?

Interview Exercise

If you prefer to interactively work with an individual or group on creating your Mission Statement, have an interviewer ask you these questions, and have them write down your responses. Use the right column to restate what the interviewer heard, in your words.

The Interviewer	You
1. Why will clients/customers use your services or products?	Answer restated:
2. What is your business or organization committed to providing your clients?	Answer restated:
3. What is the promise your company makes to its customers/clients?	Answer restated:
4. What passion(s) are you trying to satisfy by building this business?	Answer restated:

More Sample Mission Statements

Listed below are sample Mission Statements for Profit Centers, Departments, Projects and Programs. Notice how each describes one or more benefits for the ultimate client or customer.

Profit Centers

These are short, customer centric (internal or external) and benefit oriented Mission Statements.

Dealer Auto Parts Dept.	Our job is to always have the Right Parts!
Plumbing Services Div.	Fast, Reliable, Worry-free Plumbing Services
Coffee Kiosk at Bookstore	Coffee, Cookies and Books...make customers happy!

Department Samples

These are highly memorable and describe why these business functions exist.

Sales	Find Customers... Close Contracts!
Marketing	Find Markets... Create Demand
Human Resources	Attract, Develop and Retain the Right Workforce.
Finance	Fund the company, Keep it Profitable

Programs/Projects Samples

These Mission Statements are eight words or less, memorable and describe the benefits these Programs and Projects will deliver.

Corp. Diversity Program	Living and Working Together... Differently!
Critical Care Software	Eliminate life-threatening errors!
Profit Improvement Program	Find & Eliminate Waste... $100,00 at a time!
Expanded Employee Benefit Program	Protection for the people that matter the most.
Publicity Project	Capture the eyes and ears of the entire Architecural World

Feedback Exercise

Review your Mission Statement on page 41 or 43 and the examples on pages 40 and 45. Is yours too long? Unclear? Refine your Mission Statement below and then discuss it with at least two people. Use their feedback to complete your final version.

Use the examples on the preceding pages to help you refine your Mission Statement:

First Person Feedback | Second Person Feedback

THE ONE PAGE BUSINESS PLAN

Next Steps for Your Mission Statement

 REVIEW: Does your Mission Statement answer these questions?

MISSION STATEMENT QUESTIONS:	YES/NO
Who will we serve?	
What are we committed to providing?	
What promise are we making?	
Describe the wants, needs, desires or problems our product/services solve?	

 REFLECT: Assuming the reader knows nothing about your business, does your Mission Statement clearly answer the question: *Why does this business exist? Is it compelling? Does it truly describe why you are building this business?*

3 **SHARE:** After reflecting on your Mission Statement for a few days, consider sharing your Mission Statement with at least a couple of people and asking them for feedback.

4 **COMPLETION!:** Satisfied with your Mission Statement? Go to the CD at the back of the book, find The One Page Business Plan template in the Forms and Templates folder, and type your Mission Statement into the template.

VISION
MISSION
OBJECTIVES
STRATEGIES
ACTION PLANS

Objectives

What business results will be measured?

"Be specific in your goal-setting!

Use your goals to drive your behavior!"

Objectives are short statements that define business success. Good Objectives are easy to write and are instantly recognizable. They answer the question "What business results will we measure?"

Objectives clarify the business results you want or need to accomplish in specific, measurable terms. For an Objective to be effective, it needs to be a well-defined target, outcome or result that can be charted or graphed over time. It is important to include different types of Objectives that cover the entire scope of your business.

Well-conceived Objectives:

- Provide a quantitative pulse of the business
- Focus resources towards specific results
- Define success in a measurable manner
- Give people/organizations specific targets
- Establish a framework for accountability and incentive pay
- Minimize subjectivity and emotionalism
- Measure the end results of work effort

Although there is no magical number of Objectives, a One Page Business Plan can accommodate nine. Consider two to three Objectives for sales or revenue, one for profitability, two or three for marketing and one or two that are process oriented.

A Simple Formula for Writing Objectives...

> *Action to be Taken*
> +
> *Graphable Result*
> +
> *Completion Date*

Here are some examples using this formula:

- Increase Sales from $120 million to $300 million over the next three years.
- Achieve Profit before Tax of $1.8 million in this fiscal year.
- Reduce Cost of Goods Sold from 43% to 38% of Sales by June 30th.
- Increase monthly units sold from 5,000 to 7,500 by August 30th.
- Increase billable hours from 600 to 750 per month by September 30th.
- Increase # of active clients from 46 to 60 by year end.
- Add 110 new clients this year; 40 in 1st half, 30 in Q3 & 40 in Q4.
- Increase average sales ticket from $5.25 per customer to $7.10 by Nov. 15th.
- Reduce Credit Line from $15 million to $11 million over the next 120 days.
- Decrease average shipping time from 5 days to 3 days by October 31st.
- Reduce employee turnover from 22% to less than 10% by 6/30.
- Increase percent of internal promotions from 10% to 20% over next two years.

It's easy to craft meaningful Objectives when you use these 5 simple guidelines:

- Objectives are GRAPHABLE BUSINESS RESULTS.
- Include numerical value in every Objective (note, not all Objectives are dollars).
- Use of "from _____ to _____" statements helps to give time & growth perspective.
- Assign a name (when appropriate) & date to assure accountability.
- Objectives included in your One Page Plan are most critical to your success.

Numbers within Numbers

Making sense of the all of the numbers within your business can be very challenging. Setting objectives and goals for the critical results in your business like sales, number of customers and profit, is difficult for most of us

So let's make it simple! In your business you have Activities and Outcomes. If you want to achieve a particular goal, you must do something (Activity). Each of those activities has a result. Let's call those Outcomes. Define the right set of Activities and their Outcomes for your business and you have formulated your recipe for success. You have also defined the right work to be done!

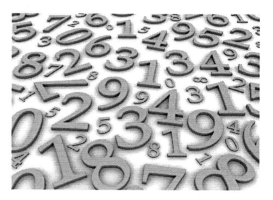

I call this the process of defining the "numbers within numbers". Every critical number or result in your business is a combination of other numbers. These numbers are almost always a combination of activities and outcomes.

In setting goals or objectives you have three choices. You can set goals for 1) activities, 2) outcomes or 3) results (activity count x outcome/activity). As you review the sample plans throughout this book you will see they are generally a combination of activities, outcomes and final results.

Let's look at the numbers within numbers for sales as an example. There are number of transactions, units sold, retail price, discounts, etc. Then there are the number of stores, websites, sales associates, wholesalers and distributors who are actually making the sales.

Stuck? Having trouble estimating sales for next year? Or in 3 to 5 years? Here is a real story about how applying the concept of "numbers within numbers" worked:

> *Food company executive was struggling with estimating how big her gourmet food company would be in five years. When I asked her to estimate sales for this year she intuitively took the number of stores her products are in and multiplied by the average sales per store per month times 12. (16 stores x $10,000/store/year). Then I asked how many stores could she envision her products being in at the end of five years. She said she did not know. I asked is 10,000 stores possible, the instant response was No! 5,000 stores? No! 1,000 stores? No! 500 stores? Response was maybe. 250 stores? That sounded doable. 250 stores x $10,000 per store = $2,500,000. That is the number this executive decided made sense to include in her Vision Statement...at this time. Obviously over time it will get refined.*

In this executive's case, her two critical "numbers within numbers" for sales are the number of stores and average monthly sales per store. Much of her plan revolves around these two numbers.

If you get stuck or confused estimating any of the critical numbers in your business, stop... then begin thinking about the numbers within the number you are trying to estimate. Break the critical number into 1) activities and 2) outcomes. Test out various values on the activities and outcomes until you feel your estimate is pretty good. This is not guessing, this is estimating the way the pros do it. Try it, over time it will become much more natural and you will become a lot more confident about your numbers.

Objectives Must be Graphable

The One Page methodology makes writing Objectives simple: All Objectives must be graphable!

We learn early in our careers that what we measure is what gets improved. If you are serious about growing a profitable business that is cash flow positive, then chart your critical success factors. Have a chart for sales, profit, # of clients, average sales price, units produced, cost of goods or services... whatever you know is critical for your success.

Charts are great... everybody can read charts. It's obvious when you are ahead of goal or not!

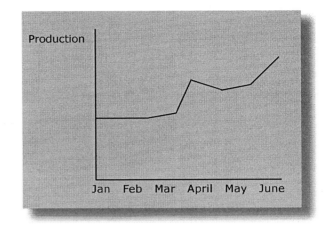

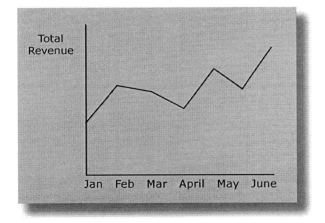

The key to setting meaningful Objectives is to identify goals that are:

- critical to your success and
- can be easily tracked
  (*Easily tracked = data is readily available and the specific target can be counted*)

Stated very simply, if you can not count or graph it over time (easily)... it's not an Objective.

On the Crafting Objectives exercise (page 54 - 59), we provide you with a number of frequently used Objectives... please note, all of them are graphable!

Microsoft Excel template for Scorecarding is on CD.

What does your Company Need More of Over Time? Less of?

Smart Objectives are Graphable Business Results! Use these graphs to brainstorm what your business needs MORE and LESS of over time in order to move to the next level of success. It is likely these are the things you will want to write Objectives for!

What does your Company need MORE of over time?

Examples:

- Sales
- Profit
- Higher Margins
- New Customers
- Repeat Customers
- Dollars/Sale
- Sales/Employee
- Production Yields
- Happy Employees

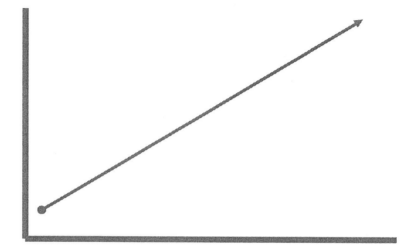

What does your Company need LESS of over time?

Examples:

- Lost sales
- Product Complaints
- Inactive customers
- Unhappy clients
- Downtime
- Excess Inventory
- Debt
- Employee turnover
- Missed Opportunities

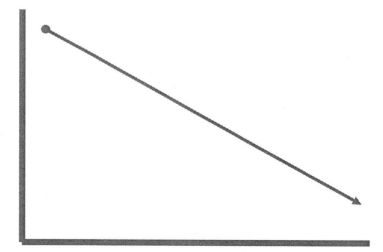

Crafting Objectives for...

We think starting with a blank piece of paper is a silly idea. There is no great mystery to writing a solid set of Objectives for your company... in fact, there is actually a formula or pattern. The four categories of Objectives and the fill-in-the-blank templates below are designed to help you think about your business from a holistic perspective... and to teach you how to write simple, clear and precise Objectives.

Financial

Total Sales or Revenues
Achieve total sales/revenues of $ _____ by 201____ .

Gross Profit
Increase gross profit margin from _____ % to _____ % by _____ .

Operating Expenses
Limit (reduce) monthly operating expenses to $ _____ ; or _____ % of sales.

Cash/Credit Cards/Credit Line/Debt
Build (maintain) cash reserves of $ _____ ; Limit credit card/debt to max of $ _____ .

Owner Compensation
Increase owner's monthly salary from $ _____ to $ _____ by _____ .

Profit before Tax
Increase profit before tax from $ _____ in 201____ to $ _____ in 201____ .

Customer

New or Active Clients
Increase number of new/active clients from _____ to _____ by _____ .

Units Sold (products, projects, programs, billable hours)
Increase number of _____ sold from _____ to _____ by _____ .

Average Revenue per Sale
Increase average revenue per sale/client/project from $ _____ to $ _____ .

Inquiries/Initial Trials
Increase # of _____ per month from _____ to _____ by _____ .

First Purchases/Repeat Purchases
Increase # of _____ per month from _____ to _____ by _____ .

Customer Service
Increase (decrease) _____ from _____ to _____ by _____ .

Startups & Small Businesses

Step 1: Review Objectives templates and mark those that seem appropriate for your business.
Step 2: Open your OPBP Word doc.
Step 3: Craft up to nine Objectives using fill-in-the-blank templates selected below.
Note: Not all of these templates will be appropriate for your business... nor is this an exhaustive list.
See pages 54 - 59 for more sample templates.

Process Improvement

Marketing (web hits, public speaking, articles)
Increase # of _____ per month from _____ to _____ by _____ .

Sales (appointments, proposals, close rate)
Increase # of _____ per week from _____ to _____ by _____ .

Manufacturing (yields, waste, quality, cost, safety)
Increase (decrease) _____ from _____ to _____ by _____ .

Operations/Services (quality, accuracy, timeliness, cost)
Increase (decrease) _____ from _____ to _____ by _____ .

Finance/Accounting (invoicing, a/r collections, payable)
Increase (decrease) _____ from _____ to _____ by _____ .

HR (new hires, training hours, overtime, # of employees)
Increase (decrease) _____ from _____ to _____ by _____ .

Learning & Growth

Output per Employee (sales, units produced, people served)
Increase _____ per employee from _____ to _____ by _____ .

Waste/Inefficiencies/Losses (time, materials, lost opportunities)
Decrease _____ waste/loss per month from _____ to _____ by _____ .

Resource Utilization (equipment, facilities, technology)
Increase _____ productivity/utilization from _____ to _____ by _____ .

Skills, Capabilities & Capacity
Increase _____ skills/capability/capacity from _____ to _____ by _____ .

Achievement (promotions, awards, recognition)
Increase _____ from _____ to _____ by _____ .

Owners, executives and managers tell us these templates help them craft clear and precise Objectives. Templates are meant to be models, not necessarily the precise wording or unit of measure. Some Objectives will use dollars, percents, units, days outstanding, etc.

Financial

Revenue/Sales: Total Company, Division, Department, Product Line, Program
Increase _____ sales from $_____ to $_____ in (month/qtr, year).

Profitability: Gross Margin, Operating Profit or Pre-tax Profit
Increase _____ profits from $_____ to $_____ (or % of sales).

Expenses: Cost of Goods/Services Sold, Operating Expenses, Bad Debt
Reduce _____ expense from $_____ to $_____ by _____ (date) (or % of sales).

Assets: Inventory, Accounts Receivables
Increase/decrease/maintain _____ levels from $_____ to $_____ by _____ (date).

Liabilities: Credit Line, Accounts Payable, Debt
Reduce _____ levels from $_____ to $_____ by _____ (date).

Customer

Number of Customers/Clients: New, Active, 1st Time Purchases
Increase number of _____ from _____ to _____ by _____.

Units Sold: Products, Cases, Billable Hours, Projects
Increase number of _____ sold from _____ to _____ by _____.

Average Sale: Dollars, Units, Profit
Increase average _____ from $_____ to $_____.

Frequency: Repeat Purchases, Referral Rate, Client Retention
Increase _____ from _____ to _____ by _____.

Quality: Customer Service, Complaints, Warranty Rate, Fulfillment Time
Increase (decrease) _____ from _____ to _____ by _____.

Businesses with Departments

Balanced Scorecard categories are designed to help you think about your business holistically and clearly define outcomes/results which are critical to your success. Note: Not all departments will have Objectives from all four categories... or need 9 Objectives.

Process Improvement

Marketing & Sales: Frequency/Effectiveness of Outreach, Responses, Success Rates
Increase (decrease) _____ from _____ to _____ by _____.

Manufacturing & Operations: Cycle Time, Yields, Waste, Quality
Increase (decrease) _____ from _____ to _____ by _____.

Finance, HR, Legal: Process Time, Quality, Effectiveness, Cost
Increase(decrease) _____ from _____ to _____ by _____.

Management & Decision Making: Process Time, Success/Failure Rates
Increase(decrease) _____ from _____ to _____ by _____.

Technology/Innovation: Time to Complete, Cost, Return on Investment
Increase(decrease) _____ from _____ to _____ by _____.

Learning & Growth

Output per Employee:
Increase _____ per employee from _____ to _____ ($, %, numerical value).

Resource Utilization: Equipment, Facilities, Technology
Increase _____ productivity/utilization from _____ to _____ by _____.

Waste/Inefficiencies/Losses: Time, Materials, Opportunities
Decrease _____ waste/loss per month from _____ to _____ by _____.

Skills, Capabilities & Capacity:
Increase _____ skills/capability/capacity from _____ to _____ by _____.

Achievement: Promotions, Awards, Recognition
Increase _____ from _____ to _____ by _____.

focus
EXERCISE

More Objectives...

On these two pages are another set of templates designed around the core business development processes of Marketing and Sales. These lists are more expansive and provide more choices for your consideration as you are developing your plan. Reminder: Your One Page Plan has the capacity for a total of nine Objectives. We also include some Personal/Well-Being Objectives for consideration.

Marketing

Contacts
Increase # of contacts per day from _____ to _____ by _____.

Appointments
Increase # of appointments per day from _____ to _____.

Presentations
Increase # of presentations per week from _____ to _____.

Closes
Increase # of closes per week from _____ to _____.

New Clients
Increase # of ideal clients from _____ to _____.

Public Speaking
Give at least _____ presentations in 1st half of 201____; _____ in 2nd half.

Publishing/Articles
Commit to writing _____ articles per quarter in 201____.

Special Events
Increase # of special events from _____ to _____ by _____.

Seminars/Educational Events
Increase # of seminars/workshops from _____ to _____ by _____.

Tradeshows/Conventions
Generate _____ prospects by attending _____ tradeshows/conventions in 201____.

Direct Mail Programs
Increase # of direct mail programs from _____ to _____ by _____.

COI - Center of Influence
Increase # of active COI's from _____ to _____. Meet with _____ COI's per month.

Sales, Marketing and Personal

Sales

Sales/Revenue per Month
Increase sales/revenue from $ _____ to $ _____ by _____.

Product Sales
Increase _____ product sales from $ _____ to $ _____ (or units).

Project/Program Sales
Sell _____ projects or programs at $ _____ for a total of $ _____.

Professional Service Sales
Sell _____ engagements at $ _____ for a total of $ _____.

Average Sale: Dollars, Units, Profit
Increase average _____ from $_____ to $_____.

Revenue per Client
Increase revenue per client from $ _____ to $ _____ by _____.

Average Engagement/Billable Hours
Increase average engagement from $ _____ to $ _____ by _____ (or hours).

Personal/Well-Being

Exercise
Increase exercise sessions per week from _____ to _____.

Weight
Decrease my weight from _____ to _____ by _____.

Vacation/Free Time
Commit to _____ weeks of vacation this year; _____ days of free time.

Community Service
Increase (decrease) total hours of community service from _____ to _____.

Personal Net Worth
Increase personal net worth from $ _____ to $ _____ by _____.

Sample Objectives

Here are six sets of Objectives from six very different companies. In these examples there are 6 to 8 Objectives that describe "what these companies will measure each month over the next 12 months to determine if they are on track." Some of these Objectives are rather traditional, others are a little unique. We hope they will get you to think creatively about your business... and what counts.

Amy Faust Wearable Art

- Grow sales to $8 million in 2011 and $12 million in 2012.
- Increase profitability to 50% of sales by July 31.
- Introduce 30 new jewelry products by January 31.
- Reduce direct costs by 40% through outsourcing manufacturing.
- Secure 6-8 catalog contracts with minimum orders of $250,000 by Sept 30.
- Register & attend 6-8 high end retail shows yearly & 2-3 wholesale shows.
- Reduce turnaround time for orders under $5000 to 3 wks. & large orders to 4-6 wks.
- Commit to 8 wks off per year and weekends when shows are not scheduled.

The Emergency IT Doctors

- Achieve 2011 sales of $500,000.
- Earn pre-tax profit of $60,000 after paying expenses and 3 principal salaries of $100,000.
- Increase number of active clients from 100 to 150 by June 30th.
- Reduce average client downtime from 6 hours to 4 hours.
- Reduce crisis response time from 2 hours to 1 hour.
- Increase percent of clients on remote technical service support program from 38% to 65%.
- Secure 150 PC audits in first six months of year to assure 33% conversion ratio.
- Reduce average OT from 26% to 10% by supplementing permanent staff w/ qualified temps.

Colorado Garden Window Company

- Achieve 2011 sales of $17 million.
- Earn pre-tax profits in 2011 of $1.5 million.
- Target Cost of Goods Sold at 38% of sales.
- Reduce inventory levels to 3.3 months on hand by August 31.
- Grow Garden Window Division at 8% per year & achieve $5.3M this year.
- Expand skylight/custom window product lines; grow sales to $7.5 million this year.
- Implement profit improvement programs & reduce product costs to 38%.
- Achieve 98% on time delivery with 98% order accuracy by 1st quarter.

There are several things to observe in these samples. Not all of the Objectives are financial, not all of them have dollars; however, all of these were first drafted using the fill-in-the-blank templates... and then edited. Also notice, all of these Objectives fit on a single line and there is only one "business result" per Objective.

Fresno Film Studio

- Raise initial $2 million capital to build a sound stage film studio by Sept. 2011.
- Generate $150,000 on-going operating budget for student film productions annually.
- Recruit 100 liberal arts students into 4-year film study program by Sept. 2012.
- Evaluate program goals with student pre-eval (Sept) and post-eval (June) annually.
- Achieve 100% participation of film students in annual Slick Rock film festival.
- Place 70% of students into summer film workshops at SF Academy of Arts.

The Financial Designers

- Increase estate planning service fees from $725,000 to $900,000 in FY2011.
- Acquire an additional 75 target clients with average estate of $2 million.
- Acquire 12 new clients with minimum net worth of at least $5 million each.
- Achieve 98% retention of recurring maintenance fees w/ existing clients.
- Create minimum of one media exposure per month, per community. Total exposures 150.
- Increase average fee per plan from $8,500 to $10,000.
- Increase total earnings per partner after expenses from $135,000 to $160,000.

Alzheimer's Care Clinic

- Provide services to 350 individuals who have Alzheimer's or a related dementia.
- Provide case management services to 180 individuals in Tri-County area.
- Provide Ombudsman services in Tri-County; 4,800 contacts with residents.
- Operate the Tri-County Adult Day Support Center at 35 average daily census.
- Operate the Metro Adult Day Support Center at 26 average daily census.
- Serve 110,000 meals through the Meals on Wheels Program.
- Increase fee-for-service revenue to $525,000; 25% above last year.
- Obtain additional $125,000 in Foundation funding.

Feedback Exercise

Share your Objectives with at least two other people. Ask them if these are the most important things for you and your team to track and monitor throughout the year. Use their feedback to fine-tune your Objectives.

First Person Feedback	Second Person Feedback

Next Steps for Your Objectives

1 **REVIEW:** Do your Objectives answer these questions?

OBJECTIVE QUESTIONS:	YES/NO
Define the most critical business results you must achieve to be successful?	
Is each Objective graphable?	
Are these Objectives realistic? Achievable?	
Keep you, your team & resources focused on the most important outcomes & results?	
Do you have the date, systems & commitment to track these Objectives?	
Establish framework for accountability & incentive pay/bonus programs?	
Is each Objective owned by someone? Have a specific achievement date?	

2 **REFLECT:** Assuming the reader knows nothing about your business, do your Objectives clearly answer the question: *What are the critical business results we must achieve to be successful?*

3 **SHARE:** After reflecting on your Objectives for a few days, consider sharing them with at least a couple of people and asking them for feedback.

4 **COMPLETION!:** Satisfied with your Objectives? Go to the CD at the back of the book, find The One Page Business Plan template in the Forms and Templates folder, and type your Objectives into the template.

VISION
MISSION
OBJECTIVES
STRATEGIES
ACTION PLANS

Strategies

How will this business be built?

Success is rarely an accident. It is usually the result of executing a carefully crafted set of strategies. Strategies provide a blueprint or road map for building and managing a professional practice or a company. They also provide a comprehensive overview of the company's business model and frequently say as much about what the company will not do, as what it will do.

Strategies set the direction, philosophy, values, and methodology for building and managing your company. They establish guidelines and boundaries for evaluating business decisions. Following a predefined set of strategies is critical to keeping your professional practice on track.

One way of understanding strategies is to think of them as industry practices. Each industry has its leaders, its followers and its rebels; each has their own approach for capturing market share. Pay attention to the successful businesses in your industry and you can learn important lessons. You can also learn a lot from the failures.

Strategies are not secret. In fact, they are common knowledge and openly shared in every industry. Pick up any industry's publications and you will know precisely what the industry's leaders have to say about the opportunities and how to capitalize on them. These leaders will also share their current problems and their solutions. This is critical information for building and managing your business. Capture the best thinking/best practices from your industry leaders along with your creative ideas that will make your company unique and you will have a powerful set of strategies that drive you and your company forward!

In summary, Strategies are broad statements, covering multiple years that:

- Set the direction, philosophy, values
- Describe ideal clients, and how you will attract them
- Define your products, services and business model
- Establish guidelines for evaluating important decisions
- Set limits on what your company will do or will not do

A Simple Formula for Writing Strategies...

> *Business-building activity or goal*
>
> +
>
> *How it will be done*

Here are a number of well-crafted Strategies using this simple formula:

Business Building Activity or Goal	How the goal will be accomplished
Become nationally known	thru public speaking, articles & media relations.
Attract young families	thru seminars, workshops & referrals.
Promote initial trial	thru in-store/restaurant tastings, coupons & advertising.
Generate repeat sales	w/ loyalty programs, monthly specials & limited promotional items.
Expand client base	by co-marketing w/ CPA's, attorneys & financial advisors.
Use special events	to attract new customers & cross/up sell to existing clients.
Use Internet	for awareness, credibility, building email list.
Attract & retain key employees	by being industry leader & known as fun place to work.
Minimize personal time on admin	thru use of virtual assistant & smart technology.
Exit business in 10 years	by selling to partners, merging w/ national firm or strategic partner.

Many people get confused about the difference between Objectives, Strategies and Action Plans. Over the next few pages we are going to help you understand the difference and make it very easy for you to craft a set of Strategies that answer these two critical questions:

- How will you build this business?
- What will make this business successful over time?

If you get confused, come back to this page and review the Simple Formula for Strategies and these examples.

What will make this business successful over time?

There are many moving parts to a successful business. There are a lot of decisions to be made. Many of the decisions are personal preference.

Keep in mind that nobody gets all the parts and pieces in place before they start. It takes time, probably three to five years. Review this list; use it as a catalyst to think about what will actually be necessary to make your business successful over time. As you are crafting your Strategies on pages 72 and 73, refer to this page.

☐ Personal expertise, energy & passion	☐ Quality control systems
☐ Previous business success	☐ Financial/Accounting controls & systems
☐ Marketing, sales & technical knowledge	☐ Business plan & budget
☐ Compelling product or service	☐ Legal & HR advisors
☐ Clear & compelling value proposition	☐ Business office
☐ Understand current market conditions	☐ Computers, software & support
☐ Ability to self-fund or raise capital	☐ Administrative support
☐ Solid reputation in industry/community	☐ Insurance coverage
☐ Ability to form strategic alliances	☐ Health, benefit, retirement programs
☐ Compelling brand	☐ Licensing & franchising
☐ Strong product name(s)	☐ Public speaking & publishing
☐ Clear pricing policy	☐ Employees or Subcontractors
☐ Trademarks/Patents	☐ Personal mentor/coach/advisor
☐ Effective sales & marketing systems	☐ Family Support
☐ Customer service support systems	☐ Peace of Mind
☐ Professional website	☐ Free time
☐ Reliable source for products/services	

Researching Strategies Appropriate for Your Business:

Finding appropriate strategies for your business is not difficult. Information is readily available to you for free or at minimal cost.

There are multiple professional, industry, trade and community associations that serve your niche. Ask other people in your line of business where they go to learn the latest trends in your industry. Go online and explore.

Be careful! The amount of information can be overwhelming. The key question is: Which strategies will you select that will be appropriate for your business? Listen to your intuition and check out what you learn with other business professionals you trust. Then craft them as Strategies and put them into your plan.

Where Does Success Come From?

Where does success come from? What will it look like in the future? Think about your past experiences and what you have learned from them. Have a friend, associate or advisor ask you these questions and record your responses.

Where have you been successful in the past? Where has your business been successful in the past?

How can you expand upon these successes?

What were your past mistakes? Mistakes your company or organization has made?

What have you learned from these mistakes?

What ideas have you not acted on?

Which of these ideas will you go forward with?

Opportunities & Threats

Review the last three issues of your industry's trade, professional or association journals and answer the questions below.

What and where are the opportunities?	How can you capitalize on them?

What threats exist?	How can you minimize the threats and/or turn them into opportunities?

Strategies for 2011 and Beyond

Opportunities & Trends

- Specialized products for women, Baby Boomers, ethnic groups and over 70 crowd.

- Sell your products anywhere in world w/ the web (theoretically).

- Market still loves highly creative, new products. Most still come from small businesses.

- Giant opportunities in all things green and health care.

Threats & Warnings

- Consumers are even more price conscious. Manufacturing in US will be difficult.

- Low prices do not translate to low quality. Commit to excellence.

- Someone else is doing what you are doing... do it better, faster, cheaper.

- Personal selling still trumps technology... pick up the phone.

Bend the Curve
Prioritizing your Strategies

Bend the Curve is one of the most powerful business tools in this book! And it is very visual. With just a little bit of explanation, everybody instantly understands it. This tool graphically demonstrates the critical relationship between an Objective and its supporting Strategies and Action Plan.

Here's the basic concept. Objectives are graphable business results as we learned in Chapter 5. Almost everyone wants their sales and profit graphs to go up overtime...and their costs, quality issues and lost sales charts to go down overtime. The question is, "what you can you do to significantly bend these curves either up or down...overtime?" The answer...Strategies! How do you implement Strategies? The answer...business-building projects or programs defined in your Action Plans.

You can use Bend the Curve to brainstorm how you will "bend" any of your Objectives and/or you can use this process to prioritize all the wild and crazy ways generated in your brainstorming down to 3 – 5 Strategies you are going to act on. Then you will define the key projects and programs that implement the Strategies.

Here is an example of Bend the Curve for sales growth:

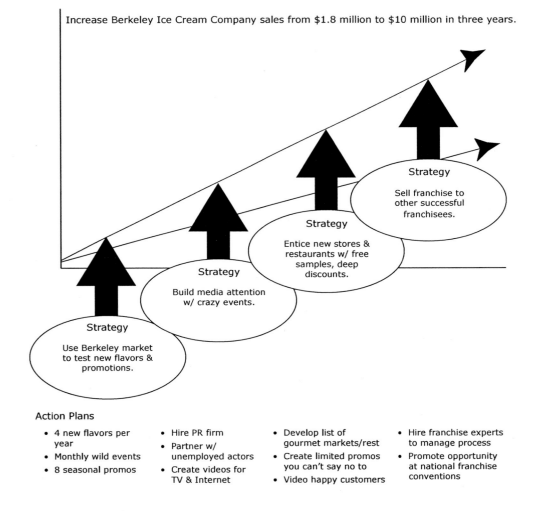

Increase Berkeley Ice Cream Company sales from $1.8 million to $10 million in three years.

Strategy
Sell franchise to other successful franchisees.

Strategy
Entice new stores & restaurants w/ free samples, deep discounts.

Strategy
Build media attention w/ crazy events.

Strategy
Use Berkeley market to test new flavors & promotions.

Action Plans

- 4 new flavors per year
- Monthly wild events
- 8 seasonal promos

- Hire PR firm
- Partner w/ unemployed actors
- Create videos for TV & Internet

- Develop list of gourmet markets/rest
- Create limited promos you can't say no to
- Video happy customers

- Hire franchise experts to manage process
- Promote opportunity at national franchise conventions

Bend the Curve
Linking Objectives, Strategies & Action
Plans

Step 1: Draft a significant growth Objective for the next 2, 3 or 5 years.

Step 2: Brainstorm up to four Strategies that are necessary to achieve the Objective in Step 1.

Step 3: Identify 2 to 4 key Action Plans per Strategy. Action Plans are typically Projects or Programs.

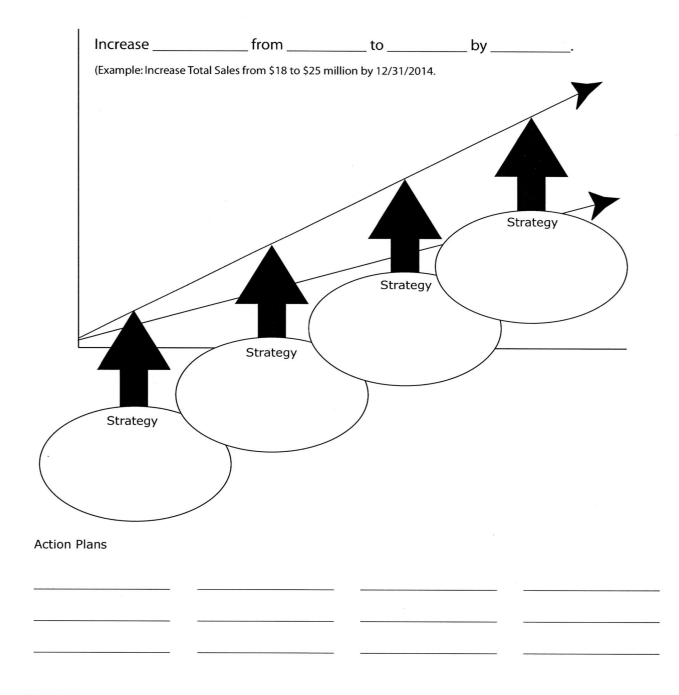

Increase _____ from _____ to _____ by _____.

(Example: Increase Total Sales from $18 to $25 million by 12/31/2014.

Strategy

Strategy

Strategy

Strategy

Action Plans

_____   _____   _____   _____

_____   _____   _____   _____

_____   _____   _____   _____

focus
EXERCISE

Crafting Your Strategies

Strategies define how you will build your business and what will make it successful over time. Owners and executives tell us these templates help them think about their business from a holistic perspective... and teach them how to write simple, but very powerful Strategies. Templates are meant to be examples and learning aids, not necessarily the precise wording.

Customer

Positioning
Become locally/nationally/internationally known for _____.

Opportunities
Focus on _____, _____ & _____ trends/opportunities.

Awareness & Initial Trial
Create awareness & initial trial by _____, _____ & _____.

Repeat Purchase
Encourage repeat purchases by _____, _____ & _____.

Promotions & Discounts
Offer _____ & _____ promotions/discounts to encourage _____.

Customer Service
Provide excellent service by _____, _____ & _____.

Process Improvement

Planning, Execution & Accountability
Strengthen _____ & _____ processes by _____ & _____.

Sales & Marketing
Improve _____ & _____ processes by _____, _____, _____.

Customers
Improve _____ & _____ customer processes by _____ & _____.

Employees
Enhance _____, _____ & _____ employee processes by _____.

Service Providers, Supply Chain, Manufacturing
Streamline _____, _____ & _____ vendor processes by _____.

Quality & Safety
Improve/expand _____, _____ quality processes by _____, _____.

Step 1: Review list of Strategies.
Step 2: Place a check mark next to those that seem appropriate for your business.
Step 3: Open your OPBP Word doc.
Step 4: Craft up to nine Strategies using templates to get started, then edit as necessary.

Learning & Growth

Industry Knowledge/Best Practices
Expand/improve _____ & _____ best practices by _____ & _____.

Communication & Presentation Skills
Improve communication/presentation skills by _____, _____ & _____.

Technology
Invest in/learn _____ & _____ technologies to improve _____ & _____.

Financial Literacy
Increase company's financial literacy by _____, _____ & _____.

Professional Development
Develop/improve _____ & _____ skills through _____ & _____ programs.

Personal Productivity
Improve personal productivity _____, _____ & _____.

Financial

Rate of Growth
Grow business at _____ % per year by _____, _____ & _____.

Profitability
Assure profitability by _____, _____ & _____.

Expense Control
Control expenses by _____, _____ & _____.

Financing
Finance business by _____, _____ & _____.

Profit Improvement
Continuously improve profitability by _____, _____ & _____.

Capital Projects
Invest in _____, _____ & _____ to support _____ & _____.

Sample Strategies

Here are six sets of strategies, from six very different companies. In these examples there are 6 to 8 strategies that describe the "essence of what will make these companies successful over time."

The HR Consulting Group

- Become known for preventing catastrophic employee problems that destroy businesses.
- Attract clients with 50 to 500 employees, business owners who want preventive solutions.
- Promote initial trial through our monthly employer council meetings & low-cost guide books.
- Generate revenues thru preventive audits & assessments, training programs & consulting.
- Use technology/Internet for tele-classes, audits & assessments, & selling training guides.
- Strategically align our firm w/ local employment law attorneys, CPAs & business consultants.
- Continue to create books, guides, audiotapes, & assessment products from existing services.
- Build a business that is ultimately not dependent on my presence; which will make it sellable.

Oklahoma Jazz Hall of Fame

- Increase revenues and surplus by promoting performances, galas & space rental.
- Build/attract membership base by promotion, advertising & organization.
- Increase revenue by offering diverse programming, increasing event frequency & mktg.
- Build donations by dev a capital campaign plan, hiring a dev consultant and a grant writer.
- Engage and educate youth by use of library, computers & practices.
- Expand scholarship endowment by corporate & individual donations & grants.
- Improve Board eff. by targeted recruiting, pre-evaluation & involvement through planning.
- Attract/retain volunteer base by membership, marketing & external programs.

Clarine's Florentines

- Promote hand-made, gluten-free, European inspired, gourmet qual. thru creative pkg/PR/web.
- Increase # of high-end gourmet stores through personal marketing & referrals.
- Promote initial trial w/ in-store demos, free restaurant trials & individual serving packaging.
- Use Internet to sell products w/ online store, promote demo locations & share stories/recipes.
- Attract media attention w/creative stories; participate in nat'l trade shows for brand visibility.
- Creatively partner w/ other small gourmet food companies; create news w/ the Sweet Mafia.
- Lease commercial kitchen & sublet to other mfg'ers to improve quality & reduce expenses.
- Have fun! Stay balanced! Have plenty of time for my new family! Enjoy life!

These strategies describe business models, best practices, culture and personal preferences. All were initially created with the fill-in-the-blank templates and then edited. Note that each strategy fits on a single line.

Portland Insurance Agency

- Become locally known for excellence in "family & business insurance solutions".
- Build long term relationships w/ prominent bus. leaders - create consistent referral source.
- Maximize visibility by serving on community, non-profit, & prof boards. Motto: Give Back Often!
- Mine existing client base for "A" clients; use seminar marketing system to find "B"clients.
- Strategic Mktg Alliances - selectively align w/ CPAs, attorneys, auto dealers, real estate profs.
- Sell thru education; use computer presentations to assure consistent message delivery.
- Staffing - hire professionals, provide quality training, 1:1 mentoring, track perf, reward Winners.

Eye 2 Eye Graphics

- Attract women business owners w/ multiple products/services & are expanding their business.
- Core Products/Services are brand strategy, design, & on-going brand support.
- Re-evaluate client process by finalizing contracts, review questionnaires & project mgmt system.
- Encourage rpt purchases w/promo pieces, project follow-up processes & using design wish lists.
- Inc public knowledge by attending events, forming partnerships, publishing articles, & speaking.
- Tgt clients/partners by updating profile, creating Ideal Partner profile & updating svc packages.
- Incr profitability by monitoring expenses, charging for extras, & updating pricing strategy.
- Inc visibility by speaking, articles in trade papers/magazines, blogging & promote e-zine.

Sarah Oliver Handbags

- Target fashion conscious women through PR and marketing campaigns.
- Target and present to new high-end gift mkts.
- Participate in sales events that highlight and honor locally made goods.
- Encourage repeat purchases via new, innovative lines and brooch customization.
- Offer samples sales 2x annually to reduce inventory and push prior season product.
- Find cost effective vendors in the areas of washing, plastic fabrication, finishing.
- Consistently improve manufacturing processes to reduce labor, materials & overhead expenses.
- Hire senior citizens for knitting to keep production local

Feedback Exercise

Share your Strategies with at least two other people that can give you their objective opinion. Ask them if this set of strategies will make your business successful over time. Use their feedback to fine-tune your Strategies.

First Person Feedback	Second Person Feedback

Next Steps for Your Strategies

1 **REVIEW:** Do your Strategies answer these questions?

STRATEGY QUESTIONS:	YES/NO
How you will build this business and what will make it successful over time?	
Describe ideal clients and how you will attract them?	
Define your products, services and business model?	
How you will Bend the Curve to achieve your key Objectives	
Define process improvements & key learnings critical to your long-term success?	
Define how your company will be financially successful over time?	
Set limits on what your company will do or will not do?	

2 **REFLECT:** Assuming the reader knows nothing about your business, do your Strategies clearly answer the question: *How will this business be built and what will make it successful over time?*

3 **SHARE:** After reflecting on your Strategies for a few days, consider sharing your Strategies with at least a couple of people and asking them for feedback.

4 **COMPLETION!:** Satisfied with your Strategies? Go to the CD at the back of the book, find The One Page Business Plan template in the Forms and Templates folder, and type your Strategies into the template.

VISION
MISSION
OBJECTIVES
STRATEGIES
ACTION PLANS

Action Plans

What is the work to be done?

"Business building projects always compete with daily fire fighting.

Allocate time and resources to the projects that will build your business."

Action Plans are business-building projects, programs and initiatives that implement your Strategies and define the critical initiatives necessary to achieve your Objectives. This is the work that must be done to build your business!

All executives and business owners struggle with the balance between "daily fire fighting" and "business-building" projects. The Action Plans you formulate should be significant business-building projects, not a list of your normal, ongoing tasks and routines. Your business plan is not your job description.

It is highly unlikely every Strategy and Objective will have an Action Plan in this plan! While this may seem counter intuitive, keep in mind your Vision, Mission and Strategies under normal circumstances reflect a multi-year perspective (3 – 5 years or more). If you are writing a three (3) year plan, the Objectives and Action Plans will reflect the three year planning horizon. If you are crafting a one year plan, the Objectives and Action Plans will focus on what you want to accomplish in the next twelve months.

If you find you have more than nine (9) Action Plans, it's possible you need to write a separate One Page Plan for one or more of the major projects... or more likely, you have defined too many projects for this year.

"Work" may be defined three ways:

- Major business building projects or programs
- Significant infrastructure projects
- Programs/Projects that bend the curves and/or trend lines

A Simple Formula for Writing Action Plans...

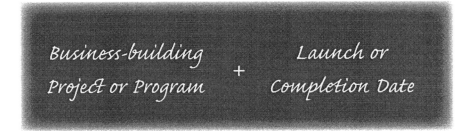

Business-building Project or Program + Launch or Completion Date

Here are some examples using the formula:

- Complete eight (8) ready-to-wear designs for trade show in Aspen by March 31st.
- Purchase and install 15 new computer aided knitting machines by July 31st.
- Introduce new packaging design & individually wrapped products by March 1st.
- Launch website w/ online store capabilities by Oct 10th.
- Complete installation of CRM system by Sept. 30th; New GL by Dec. 31st.
- Develop community outreach program (6/30). Launch in 8 metro markets.
- Hire Project Manager by April 15th to secure grant funding & construction proposals.
- Complete lease negotiations, facility rehab & move in by Oct. 15th.

Work "Bends" the Curve... Project Prioritization

In the Strategy section we used the "Bend the Curve" visual to identify the major opportunities that have the potential to significantly grow your business over the next 3 to 5 years. We can again use this visual model to help identify and prioritize the major projects and programs you and your team are going to focus on in the next twelve months.

When you have agreed on the projects that will bend the curve, assign completion dates and responsibility... then craft the Action Plans. Each of these projects is a potential candidate for your One Page Business Plan! Also be sure to calculate the expense and capital budgets for these projects and get them into your One Page Budget Worksheet, which is included in the Executive Tool Kit CD.

brainstorm
EXERCISE

Bend the Curve
Projects that Produce Results

Step 1: Craft an Objective (or use one already created) that is critical to this year's success.
Step 2: Brainstorm 2 - 4 projects, programs or actions that have potential to bend the curve.
Step 3: Identify the people, estimated expense & capital budgets required to implement projects.
Step 4: Craft appropriate Action Plan(s) with completion date(s) and personnel responsible.
Step 5: Input expense estimates and capital requirements into your budget.

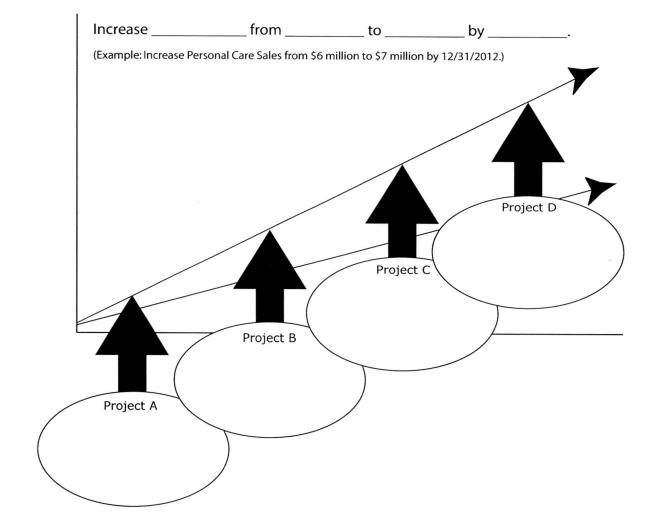

Increase _____ from _____ to _____ by _____.

(Example: Increase Personal Care Sales from $6 million to $7 million by 12/31/2012.)

Project A

Project B

Project C

Project D

Resources Required: People, Expense Budget, Capital Budget

_____   _____   _____   _____

_____   _____   _____   _____

_____   _____   _____   _____

The One Page Planning Wheel

The One Page Planning Wheel is another visual tool that helps visualize key projects over the entire year.

Most people have little problem identifying critical tasks and near-term projects that need to be completed in the next six days... or six weeks. But the identification, prioritization and calendaring of significant projects and programs in the second half of the year... or beyond, can be difficult when the focus is so often on short term results.

Use The One Page Planning wheel as a tool to brainstorm which projects and programs you are going to start, and/or complete in the next twelve months... and when you will work on them. In the brainstorming phase, identify all major projects, then refine the list down to two or three projects per quarter.

Remember, your One Page Business Plan can accommodate up to nine Action Plans.

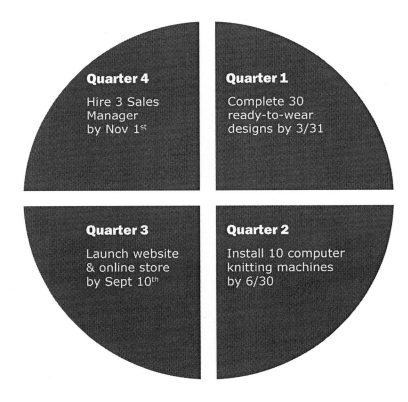

Quarter 4

Hire 3 Sales
Manager
by Nov 1st

Quarter 1

Complete 30
ready-to-wear
designs by 3/31

Quarter 3

Launch website
& online store
by Sept 10th

Quarter 2

Install 10 computer
knitting machines
by 6/30

Crafting Your Action Plans

There are four quarters in a year. List one or two major business-building projects that must be accomplished in each of the next four quarters in order to implement your Strategies and achieve your Objectives. When complete, type your Action Plans into The One Page Business Plan template that is in the Executive Tool Kit CD.

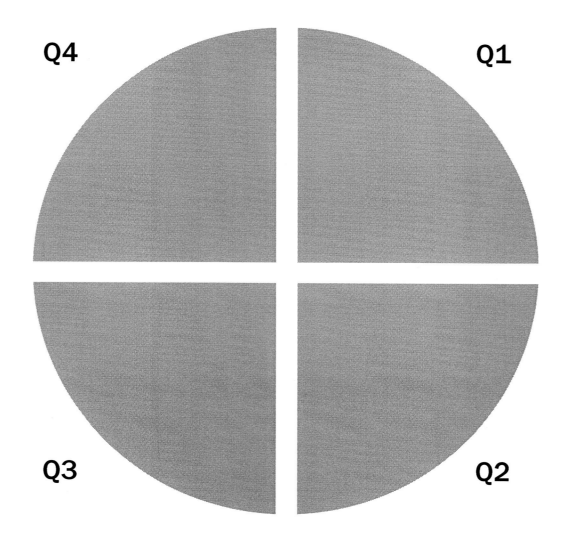

Remember: Time exists so that you do not have to do everything at once.

Feedback Exercise

Share your Action Plans with at least two other people that can give you their objective opinion. Ask them if this set of Action Plans is the right set of major projects and programs for your business to apply resources to in this next year. Use their feedback to fine-tune your Action Plans.

First Person Feedback	Second Person Feedback

Next Steps for Your Action Plans

1 **REVIEW:** Do your Action Plans answer these questions?

ACTION PLAN QUESTIONS:	YES/NO
Major business-building projects?	
Significant infrastructure projects?	
Programs/Projects that bend the curves and/or trend lines?	

2 **REFLECT:** Assuming the reader knows nothing about your business, do your Action Plans clearly define the specific actions necessary to implement Strategies and to achieve the Objectives?

3 **SHARE:** After reflecting on your Action Plans for a few days, consider sharing your Action Plans with at least a couple of people and asking them for feedback.

4 **COMPLETION!:** Satisfied with your Action Plans? Go to the CD at the back of the book, find The One Page Business Plan template in the Forms and Templates folder, and type your Action Plans into the template.

Assembling and Polishing the Plan

> *"Congratulations! Your plan is now in writing.*
>
> *Step back, review it with others.*
>
> *Refine it until it represents your best thinking."*

Assemble Your Plan onto One Page!

Select one of The One Page Business Plan templates from the Executive Tool Kit CD and type in each of the five elements of the plan you created using the various exercises.

Step Back and Review Your Plan

How does it look to you? If you are like most people, some parts of your plan will be complete, while other parts will still need editing and additional detail. Don't rush the process! Make the obvious changes now, but allow some time to reflect on your plan.

Carry the plan with you; it's only one page! As new ideas and insights appear, capture them on paper. Review the Polishing and Edit suggestions on the next page. Most people find it takes about three drafts to get their plans in solid shape... don't cut the process short. Too much depends on it.

Review Your Plan with Others

You have a plan... now review it with your partners, team, and/or trusted advisors. Have them ask you clarifying questions. Take good notes on the feedback; you might consider recording the feedback sessions. Update your plan with the feedback you decide is appropriate.

Have Partners? Employees? Have them Create their Plan

Executives, managers and employees are expensive! After you have reviewed your plan with your team, and they have had a chance to ask clarifying questions, give them 3 to 7 business days to create their One Page Business Plan. Encourage them to work together; the plans will be more cohesive as a result. Have partners? Encourage them to create their plan, then meet to review and compare plans. Make appropriate changes to bring them into alignment.

Balance and Align the Plans

Balancing the plans is a process that ensures all of the functions within your company will be working together, on the right projects and programs, in the proper sequence, at the right time... and not at cross purposes.

When your organization's plans are balanced and aligned... you can have everyone, literally, working on the same page!

Editing and Polishing the Plan

Here is a list of ideas and tips to polish your plan:

Overall Review

- Does your Vision Statement describe what you are building?
- Will your Mission Statement attract new clients? Drive employee behavior? Is it memorable?
- Are your Objectives measurable, dated and graphable?
- Do your Strategies describe what will make your business successful over time?
- Are your Action Plans significant business-building projects? Will they achieve your Objectives?

Order and Abbreviation

- Edit Objectives, Strategies, and Action Plan statements to one line.
- Eliminate all unnecessary words and phrases.
- Abbreviate words when necessary.
- Use symbols like "&" in lieu of "and" to save space.
- Use "k" or "m" for thousands and "M" for millions.
- Communicate priority of Objectives, Strategies, and Action Plans by placing them in the proper order.

Creative Considerations

- Use bullets to make key points stand out.
- Highlight key phrases in italics.

Strengthening Exercises

- Edit Vision, Mission and Strategy until they are enduring statements that "resonate"!
- Drop low-priority items. Remember, "less can produce more."
- Refine Objectives and Action Plans to be specific, measurable, and define accountability.

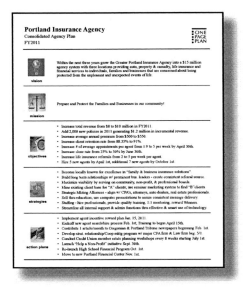

Involve Others

- Few people can write a solid plan by themselves; ask others for feedback.
- Ask your reviewers:
    - Is this plan really strategic? Too optimistic? Too pessimistic?
    - Does it include all of the critical initiatives I have been talking about?
    - Is it too risky? Too safe?
    - Does it reflect my best thinking?
    - What have I overlooked? What do you see that I missed?
- Listen to the feedback, take notes, and ask clarifying questions.
- Revise and update plan for feedback.
- Ask for another round of feedback.
- Most people find it takes at least three drafts to have a solid plan.
- Repeat until you and your reviewers agree it is solid.

Resources, Timelines and Budgets

Having a plan is critical to your success. Here are a few thoughts on other important processes that will help assure your success.

Define the Required Resources

Every project, program and initiative in your plan will need resources... or it will not happen. For each project identify the people, expenses, capital budget and any other resources required to fully execute the plan. The process of identifying the resources may cause you to realize you may not have the capability or capacity of implementing the plan you just wrote. If that is the case, go back and revise the plan.

Project Timelines

Review your project start and completion dates. Are they realistic? One of the major problems with all planning processes is the tendency to think we can do more than we actually can. When we complete a major project or initiative... we feel smart! When we have a list of projects that we have not started or are half done... we feel defeated. Take another hard look at your projects for this next year... would you be extraordinarily pleased if you completed just one or two of them? If so, adjust your plan.

Alignment with Partners & Team

If you have partners or a team, it is not unusual to find during the alignment process that the business units within your company contributing to projects and programs will not have consistent and appropriate start and completion times. For each major project or program, create an overall timeline to assure all of the sub-tasks are in alignment with the overall milestones. If project dates get changed... be sure to update the plans accordingly.

Create a Budget

Almost every activity in a business has a stream of revenue or expenses associated with it. Use your One Page Business Plan(s) to help identify all of the sources of revenue, expense and capital. If you need help in budgeting, get it. This is an important part of your success. Included in the Exrcutive Tool Kit CD is a simple One Page Budget Worksheet that should be helpful.

Recommendation: If a practice, department, project, program or company is big enough for a One Page Business Plan, it should have a separate budget.

Implementation... Tracking & Measuring the Plan

Implement Your Plan

Many plans fail because they never get implemented! When great ideas sit on the shelf... nothing happens. Put your plan to work. You can bet your competitors are working on theirs!

Monitor & Measure

Create a Performance Scorecard for each Objective. Remember: Objectives, if well written, must have a numeric value that is graphable. Included in the Executive Tool Kit CD is a fun and easy template for creating Scorecards. You can graph your results against your Objectives, your Last Year Numbers and your Forecast Numbers (if appropriate)... you will have a visual picture of all the key metrics in your company. It is very simple and easy to determine if you are ahead of target... or behind.

Monthly Business Review

Recent surveys indicate only 1 in 5 businesses have a regularly scheduled monthly business review meeting to monitor the implementation and execution of their plans.

The monthly business review is a fabulous opportunity to learn what really happens in your business each month. Do a quick review of each of the major projects... are they on track? If not, address the issues and define solutions to get them back on track.

Have a business coach, professional advisor, mentor? Make it a practice to schedule an hour with them each month to review your progress against your plan.

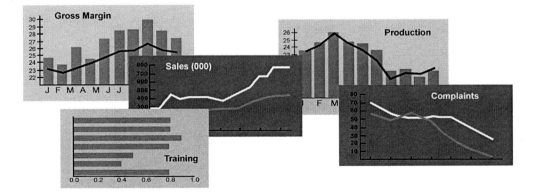

Filling in the Gaps

The process of writing a business plan, in some ways, is like writing a term paper on your business. You capture in writing what you know, conduct research to fill in the gaps, interview knowledgeable people, draft your document, ask for feedback, and then complete the final editing.

Your knowledge of your business is significant. Capture your initial thoughts in the first draft, and then begin the process of reflecting on your plan... and involving others. Keep in mind, the process of planning is one of continual reflection and refinement... and in many ways this is more important than the final document.

Most people have more resources instantly available to them than they realize. These people are very knowledgeable... and frequently free! They know you, your business, the industry, may share the same clients and may buy from the same vendors.

Over the years I have learned when I have a problem or run into a situation for the first time that is totally confusing and foreign to me the first place I turn is to my network of successful entrepreneurs, business owners and executives. They almost always have simple, practical solutions that work... and they offer them without expecting anything in return. Don't forget that your CPA, attorney, banker and vendors are excellent resources!

Other significant resources are the national and international professional trade and industry associations. All of these organizations exist to follow the trends, innovations, opportunities, regulations, etc., we need to know about, and have access to, in order to be successful. Check out their websites... better yet, pick up the phone and talk with one of the executives. Get to know the regular contributors.

One of the benefits of The One Page Business Plan is that it can be read in less than five minutes. Share your plan with your resources. Invite their insights and feedback. Your plan will be stronger!

"Your Plan is not finished until it represents the best of your thinking!"

Sample Plans...

For some, the easiest way to learn how to write a plan is to take a look at how others have written their plans. In this section we have provided several sample plans for your review.

As you review these plans, you will note that they all follow the One Page Methodology fairly closely... but not necessarily... precisely. That's OK! Each of these plans is a real plan, written by a business owner or executive. Their personal style comes through! It should... this is their business.

Note: Sample plans have these consistent characteristics

- Vision Statements paint a graphical picture of what is being built.
- Mission Statements are short, most are 8-12 words.
- Objectives are always graphable!
- Strategies describe how the company will be built.
- Action Plans describe the work to be done... all have completion dates.

Sample plans are real plans, but some of the authors requested their names, company names and locations be altered to protect their privacy.

"The One Page Plan methodology is extremely flexible.

Since 1994, over 500,000 One Page Plans have been created!"

Z-TEC, Inc. – Consolidated Plan

Jerome Johnson
CEO

vision

Within the next three years build Z-TEC, Inc. into a $2 billion global provider of integrated workflow management solutions for Fortune 1000 companies, major municipalities and significant governmental agencies at the country, state, regional and federal level. Z-TEC, Inc. will be headquartered in San Francisco with offices in New York, Dallas, London, Singapore and Rio de Janeiro.

mission

Building Industrial Strength Business Systems!

Our systems improve productivity, and reduce the costs of maintenance, materials, and facilities for large process oriented companies and municipalities.

objectives

- Achieve 2011 Revenue of at least $900 Million.
- Increase Profit before Interest & Taxes from $60 to $85 Million.
- Complete at least 300 new installations and obtain 500 new clients.
- Migrate at least 250 existing clients to Z-TEC web product cost reduction program.
- Increase Gross Margin from 51% to 55% through product cost reduction program.
- Increase sales per field employee from $250,000 to $300,000 by 9/30.
- Reduce Accounts Receivables from 60 days to 45 days.
- Achieve FTE head count of 1,500 by 11/30.

strategies

- Growth: Grow 50% each year by development of new clients and migration of existing clients.
- Reputation: Product position & strong reputation from existing client/partner referrals.
- Partnering: Align with industry leaders, partnering for marketing & solution development.
- Competitive Position: Optimize user/based pricing & modular system concepts for flexibility.
- Product Approach: Configure rather than Customize, Business Rules vs. custom programs.
- R&D: WorkFlow Solutions, Open Systems, multiple environments, Object-Oriented, flexible.
- Develop aligned team, know the plan, have sense of urgency, responsibility & accountability.
- Develop Employee Incentive Program to allow the team to share in the rewards & have fun.

action plans

- Implement Power Partner Initiatives w/Oracle UK by 3/31.
- Complete development of the Z-TEC client/server product by 3/31.
- Develop Sales & Marketing Resource Plan by 4/31.
- Develop Partner strategies w/PeopleSoft, Sun Micro, IBM by 4/30.
- Launch Europe Customer Forum in London at June 08 Convention.
- Develop Sales Force Automation Plan by August, implement in 4th Quarter.
- Implement financial reporting system at project/dept. level by Oct. 31.
- Implement professional skills development program by Nov. 30.

Z-TEC Inc. – Southern European Sales Division

Alexis Morgan
Sales Division Mgr.

vision

Within the next three years grow the southern Europe division of Z-TEC into a $150 million business unit with offices in Madrid, Barcelona, Nice and Florence.

mission

Find customers… close contracts!

objectives

- Increase sales from $35 to $45 million.
- Complete installation of 50 systems.
- Increase gross margins from 51 to 55% by increasing sale of value added services.
- Increase contribution margin to $20 million.
- Migrate at least 35 existing clients to Z-TEC internet product by 12/31.
- Reduce accounts receivable from 60 to 45 days.
- Achieve FTE head count of 275 by 9/31.

strategies

- Partners: Align with industry leaders, partnering for marketing & solution development.
- Product Approach: Configure rather than customize business rules vs. custom programs.
- Market Positioning; modular systems for flexibility, customization; premium pricing.
- R&D: Workflow solutions, open systems, multi-platform, object-oriented, flexible.
- Develop an aligned team with sense of urgency, responsibility and accountability.
- Develop employee incentive programs to allow the team to share rewards.

action plans

- Implement Power Partner Initiatives w/Oracle Spain by 5/31.
- Launch European Customer Forum in Spain at June convention.
- Develop Sales Force Automation Plan by 08/31, implement in 4th quarter.
- Implement financial reporting system at project/dept level by 10/31.
- Implement professional skills development program by 11/15.
- Complete Portugal facilities upgrades by 12/15.
- Complete communication & team performance training w/12 branch mgrs. by 3/31.

Z-TEC, Inc. – Project 6782 Printer Memory

Len Waide, Director

FY2011 Product Development Department Plan

---

vision

Develop economically viable solution to 6782 printer memory error problem by 12/1/11!

---

mission

Reduce the incidence of printer fatal error messages.

---

objectives

- Achieve .0000032 per thousand memory errors per average test cycle by Sept 1.
- Keep cost of upgrade to $1.53 per shipped unit.
- Operate within budget of $356,000.

---

strategies

- Use 3 teams of 2 engineers plus 2 outside consultants.
- Concentrate on fixing current design rather that replacing it with another.
- Hold weekly progress meeting with team to review progress against plan/budget.
- Use outside consultants on as needed basis for new laser technologies.

---

action plans

- Establish teams by 3/1.
- Identify and qualify 2 outside consultants; finalize contracts by 3/1.
- Complete problem assessment by 5/31.
- Propose an engineering solution by 6/30.
- Complete prototypes by 7/31.
- Complete product trials by 8/30.
- Document final product specs by 9/30.

Z-TEC, Inc. – Controller

Bill French, Controller, European Division

FY2011 Controller's Department Plan

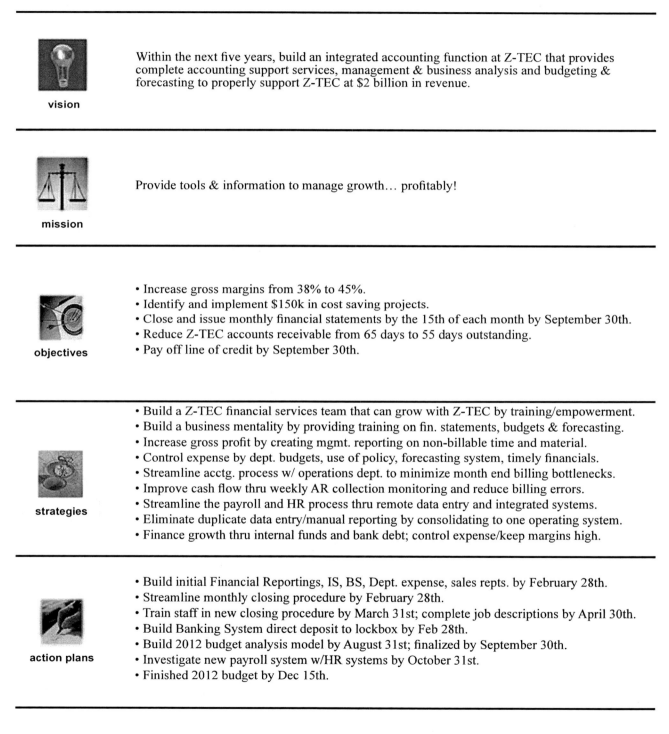

vision

Within the next five years, build an integrated accounting function at Z-TEC that provides complete accounting support services, management & business analysis and budgeting & forecasting to properly support Z-TEC at $2 billion in revenue.

mission

Provide tools & information to manage growth… profitably!

objectives

- Increase gross margins from 38% to 45%.
- Identify and implement $150k in cost saving projects.
- Close and issue monthly financial statements by the 15th of each month by September 30th.
- Reduce Z-TEC accounts receivable from 65 days to 55 days outstanding.
- Pay off line of credit by September 30th.

strategies

- Build a Z-TEC financial services team that can grow with Z-TEC by training/empowerment.
- Build a business mentality by providing training on fin. statements, budgets & forecasting.
- Increase gross profit by creating mgmt. reporting on non-billable time and material.
- Control expense by dept. budgets, use of policy, forecasting system, timely financials.
- Streamline acctg. process w/ operations dept. to minimize month end billing bottlenecks.
- Improve cash flow thru weekly AR collection monitoring and reduce billing errors.
- Streamline the payroll and HR process thru remote data entry and integrated systems.
- Eliminate duplicate data entry/manual reporting by consolidating to one operating system.
- Finance growth thru internal funds and bank debt; control expense/keep margins high.

action plans

- Build initial Financial Reportings, IS, BS, Dept. expense, sales repts. by February 28th.
- Streamline monthly closing procedure by February 28th.
- Train staff in new closing procedure by March 31st; complete job descriptions by April 30th.
- Build Banking System direct deposit to lockbox by Feb 28th.
- Build 2012 budget analysis model by August 31st; finalized by September 30th.
- Investigate new payroll system w/HR systems by October 31st.
- Finished 2012 budget by Dec 15th.

Z-TEC Inc. – Personnel Manager

Jonee Grassi, Personnel Manager

FY2011 Plan

vision

Develop a world class workforce of employees for Z-TEC International and their independent contractors who fuel the growth of the company through their creativity, dedication, and capabilities

mission

Attract, build and retain a world-class team.

objectives

- Recruit 1,600 new employees by EOY; end year with 3,600 employees.
- Decrease turnover rate from 18% to less than 10%.
- Decrease overtime from 22% to 10%.
- Increase average learning program hours/employee to 60 per year.
- Achieve internal promotion rate of 60%.
- Increase flex-scheduling optimization to 90%.

strategies

- Hire world-class team players with exceptional skill sets whenever possible.
- Retain our employees by treating them as strategic partners critical to our success.
- Commit to have resources, people & systems in place before they are needed.
- Ensure career development through innovative training & development programs.
- Highly compensate employees for their contribution; generous use of stock options.
- Support work-life balance through flex scheduling and well-being programs.
- Develop Employee Incentive Programs to allow our team to share in the rewards.

action plans

- Implement Z-TEC Employee Hiring Campaign by 01/15.
- Launch Employee Distance Learning Program by 02/01.
- Develop Intranet Flexible Scheduling facility by 04/30; implement by 9/30.
- Complete national salary survey by 06/31.
- Upgrade Kansas City national training facilities by 06/30.
- Implement professional skills development program by 11/30.

Z-TEC, Inc – Mgmt. Team Development Program

Lynne McDonald, VP Human Resources

FY2011 Plan

ONE
PAGE
PLAN

---

vision

Evolve the existing management team into a vital growing force that:
- Fuels the growth of the company by seeing and being a part of the larger vision.
- Builds on its own energy and successes; and learns from its failures/shortfalls.
- Expands its capacity to contribute to the overall management of the company.
- Develops an esprit de corps that is supportive of the individual, the team, and the company.
- Develops a manufacturing team focused on meeting the needs of the customer.
- Designs a flexible & adaptable work style/culture able to move quickly & profitably.

---

mission

Build a management team that builds the business!

---

objectives

- Improve quality of decision making (measurement TBD).
- Decrease amt of time & effort to achieve mgmt. buy-in on key projects (measurement TBD).
- Reduce average time in management meetings from 25 hours/month to 12.
- Reduce average work week for management from 60 hours to 45 hours.
- Increase internal promotion ratio from 5% to 25%.
- Decrease management turnover from 20% per year to 5%.

---

strategies

- Evolve the management team over time; do not go for immediate quick fix.
- Encourage growth and increased participation, geared to individual learning styles.
- Transfer skills from President to the mgmt. staff; provide training and coaching as needed.
- Raise collective business and financial consciousness of the team by the sharing of info..
- Allow for small errors, learn from all mistakes, and celebrate the successes!
- Minimize fanfare about the process; let team respond to positive, subtle changes.

---

action plans

- Implement business planning and budgeting process for 2012 starting in Nov.
- Design and implement financial reporting system at "level 2" by Jan. 31.
- Implement monthly business review sessions starting Feb. 20.
- Use CGC Consulting Group to facilitate quarterly "development meetings" starting 3/15.
- Implement new manager's training program in June; new supervisor's training in Aug.
- Begin development of new employee orientation learning module in Oct.
- Complete development of new employee orientation learning module by 11/15.

Colorado Garden Window Company

Mike Bozman, CEO

FY2011 Consolidated Plan

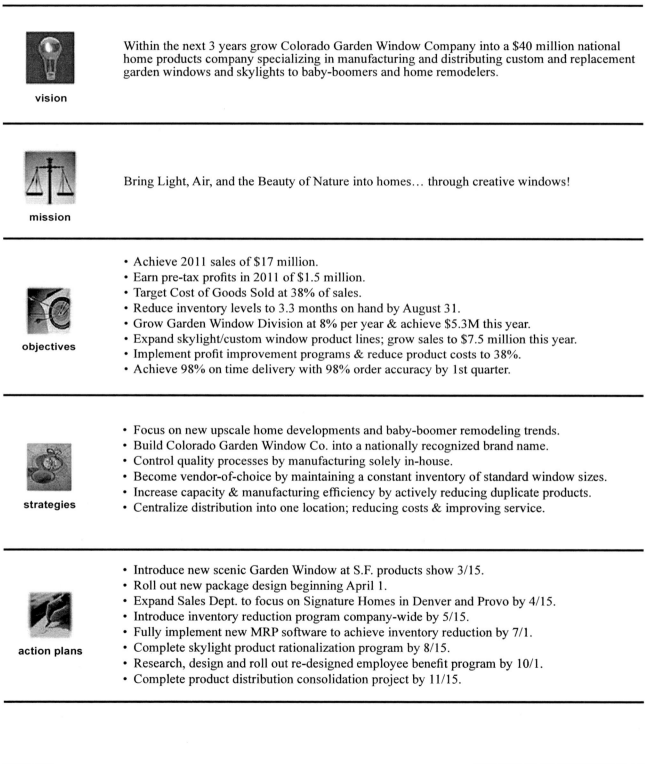

vision

Within the next 3 years grow Colorado Garden Window Company into a $40 million national home products company specializing in manufacturing and distributing custom and replacement garden windows and skylights to baby-boomers and home remodelers.

mission

Bring Light, Air, and the Beauty of Nature into homes… through creative windows!

objectives

- Achieve 2011 sales of $17 million.
- Earn pre-tax profits in 2011 of $1.5 million.
- Target Cost of Goods Sold at 38% of sales.
- Reduce inventory levels to 3.3 months on hand by August 31.
- Grow Garden Window Division at 8% per year & achieve $5.3M this year.
- Expand skylight/custom window product lines; grow sales to $7.5 million this year.
- Implement profit improvement programs & reduce product costs to 38%.
- Achieve 98% on time delivery with 98% order accuracy by 1st quarter.

strategies

- Focus on new upscale home developments and baby-boomer remodeling trends.
- Build Colorado Garden Window Co. into a nationally recognized brand name.
- Control quality processes by manufacturing solely in-house.
- Become vendor-of-choice by maintaining a constant inventory of standard window sizes.
- Increase capacity & manufacturing efficiency by actively reducing duplicate products.
- Centralize distribution into one location; reducing costs & improving service.

action plans

- Introduce new scenic Garden Window at S.F. products show 3/15.
- Roll out new package design beginning April 1.
- Expand Sales Dept. to focus on Signature Homes in Denver and Provo by 4/15.
- Introduce inventory reduction program company-wide by 5/15.
- Fully implement new MRP software to achieve inventory reduction by 7/1.
- Complete skylight product rationalization program by 8/15.
- Research, design and roll out re-designed employee benefit program by 10/1.
- Complete product distribution consolidation project by 11/15.

ZXM Automation Consulting, Inc.

Allen Marcus, President

FY2011 Consolidated Plan

ONE
PAGE
PLAN

---

vision

Within the next five years build ZXM Automation into the premier west coast industrial process automation consulting company specializing in integration solutions. ZXM Automation revenues will grow from $10 million in 2010 to $20 million by 2015 by expanding its role from a manufacturing representative company to a complete engineering field service and process solutions company.

---

mission

Helping you control your marketing, sales, service and distribution channels!

---

objectives

- Grow business 20% & achieve total sales revenues of $120 million in 2011.
- Achieve profit before tax of $15 million.
- Land at least 5 significant system projects at a minimum of $2 million each in 2011.
- Increase gross margin from 17% to 20%.
- Increase sales per employee from $320,000 to $375,000.
- Increase Engineering Services billable utilization from 50% to 70%.

---

strategies

- Sell total solutions not parts.
- Significantly increase valued added engineering & integration service capabilities.
- Expand geographically into So. Calif., Oregon/Washington, Nevada, Arizona, Alaska.
- Aggressively target niche markets in each geographic market.
- Expand thru selective acquisitions and/or strategic partnerships.
- Continually develop the discipline of profitability for ZXM & our clients.
- Attract/retain key employees by maximizing their creative, technical & business talents.
- Share growth & prosperity w/ employees through incentive & equity participation

---

action plans

- Critical Marketing Program: Visit all 25 base system clients in 2nd Q.
- Hire System Eng. by 4/30 and Sales Mgr. by 6/30.
- Implement Client Awareness & F2K Support Programs in 3rd Q.
- Complete UC Berkeley, Lipton, SAI projects successfully by 9/30.
- Implement F2K Demo website in 4th Q.
- Install new NT server by 3/31 & Unix server in 2nd Q.
- Implement Sales Automation Program and complete conference room demo in 3rd Q.
- Complete business practices, procedures & policy manual by 12/31.

California Knits

Mary Beth Miller, President

FY 2011 Consolidated Plan

vision

California Knits is a creative, soul-filled enterprise that provides:
• vibrant, unique, comfortable clothing as art for women.
• custom design capabilities for individual clients.
• training and mentoring of the next generation of machine knit artists.

Within 3 years California Knits will be a $50 million internationally recognized brand, serving the upscale fashion market for women who want to look and feel fabulous in knit clothing.

mission

Providing color, light, and energizing beauty in comfortable, natural fiber clothing.

objectives

• Achieve 2011 revenue of $28 million.
• Increase profit before tax from $1.6 million to $2.5 million.
• Achieve profit margin of 50%.
• Hold production labor to 18% starting March 15th.
• Increase active store count to 200, an increase of 30% over FY2011.
• Outsource 50% of production by 4th quarter.
• Add 10 designs; 9 ready-to-wear; 1 gallery collectible. New sales $2.5 million.
• Attend at least 12 trade/trunk shows in 2010; book $750,000 in orders.

strategies

• Attract attention with stunning gallery quality garments priced at $2,000+.
• Design ready-to-wear products at affordable price points; $75 - $200.
• Outsource ready-to-wear; reserve personal time to create gallery garments.
• Develop professional team for production and operation of business.
• Cultivate relationships with upscale clients for referrals and shows.
• Explore avenues to entertainment industry for costume and personal clients.

action plans

• Develop budget and plans for capital needs for major expansion by 2/15.
• Contact six fashion magazines; present portfolio for publication on 4/20.
• Complete 8 ready-to-wear designs for show in Aspen in May.
• Attend national trunk shows: New York, Santa Fe and Carmel; Q2 + Q3.
• Purchase and install 3 new computer aided knitted machines by 6/30.
• Complete redesign of display booths for winter fairs by 10/31.
• Complete installation of CRM system by 10/31. New GL by 12/31.

Shea Therapeutic Equestrian Center

Dana Butler-Moburg
Executive Director

vision

With the next three years, grow the Shea Center into a preeminent $2 million organization providing therapeutic equestrian activities to a diverse community of people with special needs, and providing internationally recognized education to therapeutic equestrian professionals.

mission

Improve the lives of people with disabilities through therapeutic horse-related programs.

objectives

- Expand operating campaign to $1.7 Million.
- Raise $1.5 Million through capital campaign.
- Increase annual fund to $250,000.
- Implement bilingual programming with 12 families.
- Increase community awareness by 50%.
- Raise $500,000 by June 30 through Campaign Committee leadership.

strategies

- Core services include therapeutic riding, hippotherapy, and non-mounted activities.
- Raise capital funds using new campaign committee.
- Redesign and staff annual fund and face-face giving program.
- Increase public awareness through community speaking and media relations.
- Develop campaign prospects through new Board connections.
- Maintain development focus thru weekly review mtgs.
- Develop more effective budget, cost control, reporting systems.
- Dana to be more involved in developing prospects, solicitation and stewardship.

action plans

- Implement budget & cost control program (1/15).
- Hire new business manager to take on operational responsibilities (3/15).
- Recreate Campaign Committee by (4/30).
- Develop community speaking program (6/30). Deliver monthly talks in Fall.
- Staff Board, all Committees (6/30). Board Training (Sept)
- Launch monthly development meetings (6/15); biweekly (9/15).
- Complete equestrian facility (7/31), offices (11/30).
- Recruit 5 Comm members (8/31), ID prospect list (9/30), develop new materials (9/30)

The One Page Business Plan...
Now a Best-Selling Series!

For the Creative Entrepreneur

This is the million-dollar best seller that forever changed the way people write business plans. This is the fastest, easiest way for creative entreprenuers and small business owners to write a business plan!

For the Professional Consultant

New to consulting? Need to move your practice to the next level? This book was written by consultants, for consultants. It contains everything you need to create a blueprint for a successful consulting practice... all on a single page.

For Non-Profit Organizations

If you are responsible for starting, managing or funding a non-profit... this book was written for you. One Page Plans create a community culture of discipline and accountability. This process helps executives, employees, volunteers and boards clearly define and live up to their promises.

For Financial Services Professionals

Industry leaders in insurance, banking and financial services demanded we create this special edition for their industry. If you make your living selling financial products or services or managing people that do... this book was written for you!

For the Creative Entrepreneur (Spanish Edition)

This is the Spanish language version of the million-dollar best seller that forever changed the way people write and implement business plans.

For Women in Business

Finally, a business planning book for women in business! It combines Jim Horan's proven methodology with Tamara Monosoff's experience, insights, colorful stories and real business plans from women all over the country.

Available at www.onepagebusinessplan.com/books

(For quantity pricing call: 510-705-8400)

And local bookstores, Amazon & other online retailers!

Need More? *We Can Help!*

Executives with Management or Sales Teams

Over the last nineteen years we have helped thousands of executive teams implement The One Page Business Plan Process… usually in less than four weeks! Each executive, business unit manager and project team creates their One Page Plan which is in alignment with the overall company's plan. You can then monitor results monthly with our web-based Planning and Performance System with online Scorecards and Progress Reports. Interested? Visit us on the web for a short video about this system.

Business Owners with Executive or Management Teams

There is a new breed of business owner in the marketplace today. They are starting up new businesses and reinventing established ones. They are intensely passionate, competitive and dedicated. They care about people, the environment, and their communities. They don't run their businesses casually. If you are one of those business owners, you'll appreciate the focus, discipline and results you'll achieve by implementing One Page Plans in your business. Call now or visit us on the web.

Entrepreneurs, and Venture-funded Startups

Today's small business issues are complex, resources are limited, and time is of the essence. There's no room for mistakes. You have to think fast and move faster. What this requires is an innovative, fresh approach to business planning... one designed to act as a catalyst for your ideas. The One Page Business Plan is a powerful tool for building and managing your business. It's short, concise, and it delivers your plan quickly and effectively. There can be no question as to where you are going when it's in writing!

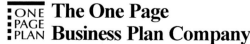

The One Page Business Plan Company

Consulting • Training • Web Based Performance Management Systems

510.705.8400 • www.onepagebusinessplan.com/women

Executive Tool Kit
How to Install and Use the CD

Installation Instructions:
Simply load the CD into your CD drive. requires Microsoft
Word® and/or Excel® to use the templates, forms and
spreadsheets. Open any Directory with a double-click.
Select desired Word® document or Excel® spreadsheet.

CAUTION:
Immediately after opening any of the files we encourage you to save
the file with a new name using the "SAVE AS" command in order
to preserve the original content of the file.

No Technical Support
This CD is provided without technical or software support. Please
refer to your Microsoft Word® or Excel® User Manuals for questions
related to the use of these software programs.

System Requirements:
Windows 95/98/NT/2000/XP/Vista
Macintosh OS 9.1 or higher
Microsoft Word® and Excel®
CD/ROM drive